Harper's Comparative Government Series

MICHAEL CURTIS, EDITOR

BRITISH GOVERNMENT AND POLITICS

Life Without a
Declaration of Independence

DOUGLAS V. VERNEY

YORK UNIVERSITY

HARPER & ROW
Publishers

NEW YORK AND LONDON

BRITISH GOVERNMENT AND POLITICS: *Life Without a Declaration of Independence* / Copyright © 1966 by Douglas V. Verney. Printed in the United States of America. All rights reserved. No part of this book may be used or reproduced in any manner whatsoever without written permission except in the case of brief quotations embodied in critical articles and reviews. For information address Harper & Row, Publishers, Incorporated, 49 East 33rd Street, New York, N.Y. 10016.

C-1

Library of Congress Catalog Card Number: 66-15676

For my mother and in memory of my father,
John Henry Verney (1884–1965):
Liberal, Nonconformist, Mancunian and Lancastrian—
one who was eminently Victorian.

CONTENTS

TABLES

PREFACE

I WOULD like to thank a number of colleagues and friends in England and Canada who read parts of the manuscript: Mr. D. S. Rickerd (Chapter 1); Mr. J. W. Grove (Chapter 3); Mr. G. V. Doxey and Mrs. Jean Bonnor (Chapter 4); Mr. Brian Chapman and Mr. Michael Goldrick (Chapter 5); Mr. Michael Lawrence (Chapter 6); Mr. Peter Bromhead (Chapters 6 and 7); and Mr. R. T. McKenzie (Chapters 8 and 9).

Two authorities on British government and politics, Sir Denis Brogan of Cambridge University and Mr. J. D. Hoffman of York University, read the whole manuscript. Mr. G. Singleton of H. M. Treasury provided figures for Tables 5.1 and 5.2. Mrs. Constance Catherwood checked a number of references for me. Mrs. Helen Allen typed the manuscript, smoothing the rough edges. To all of these I offer my thanks.

I am of course in debt to innumerable scholars who have examined the various aspects of the British political system at length. Indeed it is because there are so many sober assessments of the system that I have felt justified in offering my own transatlantic interpretation, warts and all.

DOUGLAS V. VERNEY

York University,
Toronto

PART I

Life Without a Declaration of Independence

British government and politics have long exercised a peculiar fascination over the minds of men everywhere. For three centuries Britain was the modern equivalent of Greece and Rome combined, embodying the political ideas of the one and the imperial grandeur of the other. Writers like Hobbes, Locke, Bentham, Burke, and Mill revived a great tradition of political theory begun by Plato and Aristotle. The British Empire was even more impressive than the Roman in the extent of its frontiers, the efficiency of its administration and the impartiality (insofar as an imperial authority can be impartial) of its justice. At the heart of the Empire was the United Kingdom, a country which justly prided itself on the stability of its government and the adaptability of its political system to a rapidly changing world.[1]

The British have managed to preserve their traditional institutions of Crown, Lords, and Commons despite the loss of the American colonies in the eighteenth century, the extension of the franchise in the nineteenth, the spread of socialist ideas, and the transformation of the former colonies into independent members of the Commonwealth in the twentieth. In Part I we shall be concerned with the nature of British society, more deferential than that of North America, and the principles underlying its governmental system, many of which date from before 1776 and have been barely modified since. We shall not be primarily concerned with British history—but of no country can it be said with more certainty that its present is determined by its past, and a past very different from that of the United States. To give but one example of the difference, 1776 is to Americans that annus mirabilis of the Declaration of Independence. To the British it is merely a vintage literary year, the year when, for example, Gibbon published his Decline and Fall of the Roman Empire, Adam

---

[1] *Britain: An Official Handbook, 1964* has no reference to "Empire" in its index.

Smith his Wealth of Nations, Jeremy Bentham his Fragment on Government, and Tom Paine his Common Sense.

And whereas most peoples draw a fairly sharp distinction between their prerevolutionary, or at least their preindependent, condition and their present political (and sometimes social) structure, the British almost alone have preserved continuity in their institutions, since 1066 at any rate. To understand this unusual polity it is necessary to grasp the most significant fact of British political life—that is life without a Declaration of Independence.

CHAPTER ONE

A More Deferential Society

You may not trust my word, but will you not accept the word of a British gentleman (Herbert Samuel) who has been Governor of Palestine?
Trade union leader to striking coal-miners in 1926

A Densely Populated Group of Islands

THE UNITED KINGDOM comprises the major part of the British Isles, a group of islands offshore from the great European continent. As in Japan there are a great many people—53,000,000—confined to a small area. (Ireland is part of the British Isles but the Irish Republic is not part of the United Kingdom.)

How unified are the British? It is a truism that there is much more homogeneity in Britain than there is in the United States. People may live in Scotland or Wales but they vote Labour or Conservative and there is a very marked sense of common identity vis-à-vis foreign states. Where other countries have struggled with the problem of ethnic minorities, the British seem to have concentrated their energies on the differences of social class. But it would be a mistake to pass over, as many commentators do, the differences between the peoples of the British Isles too easily, for they have been so profound as to lead to modifications in the political structure almost as significant as the introduction of federalism in the United States.

Ireland proved so intractable that after an attempt at forcible assimilation from the time of the Union of 1800 to the setting up of the Irish Free State in 1922 there had to be a gradual relinquishment of authority which ended in complete independence for the Republic of Ireland in 1949. As for Northern Ireland, although it sends representatives to the British Parliament, it has a parliament of its own operating under a system known as "devolution."

The Scots who sent their King to govern England in 1603 and formed a United Kingdom by Act of Union in 1707, have always expected to be treated as a separate nation and many of the government departments in Whitehall do not operate in Scotland. Since 1885 there has been a Secretary (of State since 1926) for Scotland; four departments in Edinburgh deal with Scottish affairs. Scottish law differs from English common law.

In 1951 the Welsh were able to secure the services of a Cabinet minister who had the additional title of Minister of Welsh Affairs; in 1964 they were awarded a Secretary of State, with full cabinet rank. But the status of Wales is lower than that of Scotland. Wales is more often treated as an integral part of England, having the same structure of local government. This is because Wales, unlike the more remote Scotland and Ireland, was considered a threat to the heart of England in the Middle Ages and thus became a conquered principality. (The proud Scots may perhaps be compared to the Texans, the Irish problem to that of Southern segregation or of Quebec. There is no possible American parallel with Wales.)

These various subtle distinctions are conveyed in the precise terms which are used to describe the islands. The geographical description of the two main islands is traditionally the *British Isles*. The political term for the parts that are governed from Westminster is the *United Kingdom*, which is short for United Kingdom of Great Britain and Northern Ireland—the Irish Republic naturally being excluded. *Great Britain* properly speaking is the main island, comprising England, Scotland, and Wales. Not many people outside government service understand these distinctions and most people use the term Britain. Some Englishmen (and more foreigners) call the whole country "England," but this is not advised except when referring to the cricket team

Table 1.1. Population (1961 Census)

England	44,018,000	
Wales (including (Monmouthshire)	2,651,000	
Scotland	5,197,000	
		Great Britain 51,866,000
Northern Ireland a	1,435,000	
		United Kingdom 53,301,000

Density of Population (per square mile)

United Kingdom	562
Japan	659
United States	51
USSR	25

a Republic of Ireland 2,818,341.

(which plays five countries of the Commonwealth and South Africa in Test Matches. Canada is sufficiently North American not to participate.)

It might be thought that the governmental structure of the British Isles would be based on the various countries [1] which compose them. It is not quite that simple. The main gulf, of course, is between the Irish Republic and the rest of the British Isles which forms the United Kingdom. Within the United Kingdom itself there is a variety of jurisdictions. Northern Ireland, which is inhabited mainly by Presbyterians whose ancestors came from Scotland, has its own government and Parliament: Scotland has its own ministry but not its own Parliament; while Wales has neither, although it now has a Secretary for Wales. Nor is this all. The Isle of Man, situated in the Irish Sea, has its own ancient Parliament called Tynwald and the acts of Parliament passed at Westminster do not automatically apply to the island, which among other things levies its own income tax at a lower rate than the mainland. Off the coast of France are the Channel Islands, partly French-speaking and occupied by the Germans during World War II. These were owned by William the Conqueror, who was Duke of Normandy, and also have their own self-government divided between Jersey and Guernsey (together with Alderney and Sark.)

Altogether, therefore, there are no fewer than eight political jurisdictions above the ordinary local government level in the British Isles: England, Northern Ireland, Scotland, Wales (which form the United Kingdom), the Isle of Man, Jersey and Guernsey (which are Crown dependencies)—and the Irish Republic, which of course is quite separate from all the others (though Irishmen can vote in parliamentary elections.) There are about 5000 islands in the British Isles, most of them uninhabited, but no other jurisdiction has contemporary political significance, though some, e.g., the Western Isles, have quaint histories.

The United Kingdom of Great Britain and Northern Ireland,

---

[1] *The Columbia Encyclopedia* carefully refers to Wales as a "peninsula," Scotland as a "political division," and Northern Ireland as an "administrative unit."

with which this book is primarily concerned, consists of the first four of these eight jurisdictions. The government at Westminster easily outranks all the others in importance, but the regional capitals—Edinburgh, Belfast, and Cardiff—should not be totally ignored. In the nineteenth century men thought of the British Empire: today as the Empire is transformed into an amorphous Commonwealth attention is turning more to the islands themselves, the variety in their political and social life, and the picture they convey of an association of people who while somehow avoiding the federal system of government have nevertheless been compelled to adopt some noteworthy alternatives in local and regional government to meet the inevitable demands for autonomy by the nations which compose them.

An Involved Evolution

It is too early to say what the consequences of the rapid dissolution of empire will be, but there are indications that the British are being thrown back increasingly on their cwn resources and are no longer the richest nation in Europe.[2] They are becoming aware more than ever of their precarious way of life in a country which can feed only half the population, and which depends for its survival as an important power upon the ability of the people to outsell their competitors in the fierce trading which characterizes the modern world. No country has been so internationally oriented, while remaining so insular, as the United Kingdom. (The British do not think of themselves as Europeans despite their attempts to talk the language of European federation.)

There is an interesting contrast between the old imperial Britain and the new island political economy, and we shall examine the ways in which the people and their government have tried to remold their nation—a nation which proudly boasts that it has

[2] By 1963 Britain's per capita product (valued at $1564) was lower than that of France ($1658), Germany ($1653), Luxembourg ($1615), Denmark ($1675), Sweden ($2046), and Switzerland ($2002).

not been conquered since 1066 and which unlike the French, the Russians, and the Americans has no revolution to mark its entry into the modern world. The British have no Independence Day; their only political celebration, oddly enough, is November 5th when bonfires are lit to celebrate the *failure* of Guy Fawkes to blow up the Houses of Parliament in 1605.

American history, like that of a number of countries which have experienced revolution, has a definite starting point for its modern political system. It matters little whether the date chosen is 1775 or 1789 or one of several dates in between; the framing of the Constitution marks a complete break with the colonial past. And though scholars recognize the many elements of continuity between the old America and the new, no one disputes the fundamental *political* difference between the thirteen colonies and the United States of America. Even the proponents of the idea of a conservative America continuing, despite war and revolution, to develop its own ethos, find that there are yet earlier and quite definite watersheds—1620 for Yankees and 1607 for Southerners.

But where are the comparable dates in British history? When can we say that the British threw off tyranny? (Unlike the Americans, they kept George III as King.) Have they not preserved the "yoke" of monarchy to this day, bearing it lightly no doubt from a conservative point of view, but permitting its social prestige to suffocate the occasional angry cries of radicals? The British, it is true, have their cut-off dates, but there is agreement only about three of them. About the third and vital one of the four, there is still debate.

The first date is 1066, the last date on which a conqueror set foot on British soil.[3] The English conveniently forget that the Normans stayed in England, and that their descendants still form the historical nucleus of the upper class. The words for various domestic animals like calf and sheep are Saxon; the terms for the cooked food the conquerors ate—veal, mutton, beef—are Norman in origin.

---

[3] The term "British" survived the Norman Conquest as it did the earlier invasions by Romans, Anglo-Saxons, and Norsemen.

Table 1.2. Economic Position

Exports 1938–1963 in Millions of Dollars [a]

	1938	1948	1963
World Exports	23,500	57,500	153,500
British Exports	2,414	6,297	11,414

Comparative Standards of Consumption in 1960 [b]

	U.K.	France	Germany	Sweden
Per capita product (dollars)	1493	1276	1263	1631
Automobiles per 1000 population	106	109	85	158
TV sets per 1000 population	209	33	76	108
Telephones per 100 population	151	91	101	354
Newsprint consumption (lbs. per person)	48.7	23.4	19	50.9

Comparative growth rates 1951–1960 (U.S.: 1950–1961) [c]

United Kingdom	2.7	France	4.5	Germany	7.1	Sweden	4.0
United States	2.7	EFTA	3.3	EEC	5.5		

SOURCE:
[a] United Nations Statistical Yearbook, 1964, Table 160, p. 465.
[b] United States Statistical Yearbook, 1963, Table 1245, p. 915.
[c] United States Statistical Yearbook, 1964, Table 1264, p. 915.

The second date is 1215 when the barons compelled King John to accede to their demands, and laid the foundations for that aristocratic society which was to be known in the eighteenth century as the Whig oligarchy, and which survives to this day as an attenuated House of Lords. Cynics may question the "democratic" character of Magna Carta, but generations of Englishmen have proudly and rightly claimed that it established their right to govern by the rule of law and not by the arbitrary whim of an autocratic monarch. (The Great Charter was confirmed by later monarchs no less than forty times in the next two hundred years.)

The fourth date is 1832, which the Victorians called the year of the Great Reform Bill. At a time when Andrew Jackson was entering the White House and spreading the radical gospel of Jacksonian democracy, a staid House of Commons and a reluctant House of Lords were giving large cities like Manchester their first representation in Parliament and extending the franchise to the prosperous middle class. Like 1215, the year 1832 was hardly revolutionary—and another century was to elapse before all adults over 21, including women, were entitled to vote—but it was an important step in Britain's involved evolution.

But England *did* experience revolution, and it is over the significance of the English Civil War which broke out in 1642 and led to the beheading of Charles I in 1649 that debate continues. For the Civil War in itself did not settle everything or indeed anything; the victors ultimately were the losers: the Commonwealth of Cromwell (1649–1658) came to an end and in 1660 Charles' son was welcomed as King Charles II. The monarchy continued and the extravagances of the court became notorious. In some ways the death of Queen Elizabeth I and with her the Tudor dynasty in 1603 had been a greater break with the past than the Civil War, and few British histories stop or start in 1642 or 1649 or 1660. Only a handful of religious Dissenters, whose descendants briefly reared their heads in the 1790s to be smartly rebuked by the great statesman Edmund Burke for reviving bitter memories of controversies best forgotten, remained loyal to the puritan and parliamentary cause. Their nearest counterparts were

Table 1.3. Some Important Dates and Periods

54 B.C.	Roman invasion
1066	Norman Conquest
1215	Magna Carta
1265	First Parliament
	1485–1603 Tudor monarchs
	1603–1714 Stuart monarchs
	1714– — Hanoverian monarchs
1642	Outbreak of Civil War
1649	Execution of Charles I
1660	Restoration of Charles II
1688–1689	"Glorious Revolution" and Bill of Rights
1713	Peace of Utrecht
1721–1742	Sir Robert Walpole first Prime Minister
	1714–1830 George I–IV
	1837–1901 Queen Victoria
	1901–1910 Edward VII
1911	Parliament Act
	1910–1936 George V
	1936– — Edward VIII
	1936–1952 George VI
	1952– — Elizabeth II
1949	Second Parliament Act

Four Phases of Parliamentary Development, Approximate Dates

1265–1603	Monarch governs and Parliament supplies money
1603–1688	Dispute of Parliament with King over supreme power
1688–1914	Evolution of parliamentary government
1914– —	Cabinet government

to be found in New England. Here there was founded a New World radicalism, also based on puritan and parliamentary principles, which was destined to triumph a century later and even to be the object of some sympathy on the part of Burke. But then he was somewhat younger. When revolution broke out in France, and of course that was a much more unseemly revolution, Burke was highly critical. The American leaders, unlike the French revolutionaries, were gentlemen.

How is it that the memories of the English Civil War should be so dim in England (though not in Ireland where Cromwell's men are estimated to have caused the terrible death of 600,000 people)? The answer is that for most people the third important date in England's constitutional history is not the Civil War's beginning or end but the year 1688—the year of the Glorious Revolution which was in fact no revolution at all. In that year the British said farewell to a surprised King James II, a Stuart who, unlike his erring brother Charles II, had been naive enough to attempt to reimpose Catholicism on England. William of Orange was asked to become King and an indifferent people witnessed yet another change in the monarchy. To those who invited him, however, the change was far more important than any which had proceeded it; indeed it spelled the end of the attempt of the monarch to rule absolutely. Just as the age of absolutism was beginning on the continent of Europe it abruptly ended in Britain, causing the British to feel a race apart, and a nation superior to the "Europeans" for centuries to come.

Yet it is a peculiar fact of English history that none of the hallowed dates in the schoolbooks can be called a victory for democracy in any meaningful sense of the term. The first, 1066, was simply a royal conquest following which England was divided up among the fortunate conquerors. The other three watersheds, 1215, 1688, and 1832 involved the nobility, whose ancestors had been William's marauding minions. It was the barons who insisted on Magna Carta; it was the Whig lords who deposed James II; and it was even lords, Lord Grey and others in the upper house, who secured the passage of the 1832 Reform bill. It was not until 1909 that Lloyd George, a fiery Welsh politician, proclaimed the cause of the people versus the peers. This time the people, or at least the Liberal party, won, but by the twentieth century it was obvious that the House of Lords, like the monarchy before it, had had its day: in 1911 the Parliament Act curbed its powers.

It is more useful to look at British history in quite a different way from American. It is better to ignore particular dates and to concentrate on certain periods, some decades long and others taking centuries. For this is what "evolution" means. Even putting dates at the beginning or end of these long phases of development is dangerous, for it would be as wrong to think of England entering a new age when the first Stuart King James I succeeded Elizabeth I in 1603 as it would be to imagine that when the news of Columbus' discovery of the New World reached Europe in 1492 all the monks sadly lamented the passing of the Middle Ages. (These, incidentally, are sometimes presumed to have ended in England in 1485 with the accession of the Welshman Henry VII as the first Tudor monarch!)

But, allowing for a certain license, four great periods in English history can be dimly discerned. The first saw the rule of the monarch, sometimes advised by Parliament (which dates from at least 1265 when counties and boroughs sent representatives) and sometimes not. Whatever the meaning of Magna Carta to seventeenth- and eighteenth-century Englishmen, until the death of Elizabeth I the right of the monarch to rule was not really questioned, though after about 1400 the King could not impose direct taxes without Parliament's consent. It was Elizabeth as Commander in Chief who defeated the Spanish Armada, not the Houses of Parliament. And it was her successor, James I of England (and VI of Scotland) the "wisest fool in Christendom," who was responsible for the splendid Authorized Version of the Bible. The preface to this begins, "Great and manifold were the blessings, dread Sovereign, which Almighty God, the Father of all mercies, bestowed upon us the people of England, when first he sent Your Majesty's Royal Person to rule and reign over us." Throughout English history from Boadicea to Elizabeth, ultimate power lay (or was supposed to lie) with the monarch.

The second phase, which began shortly after James became king in 1603 and continued until the Revolution of 1688, was an era of struggle between King and Parliament. It was also between the High Church party and the Puritans, between the court and the City of London, and between prerogative courts and common-law lawyers. The City won, as did the common-law lawyers and above all Parliament. The Puritans lost. Yet power did not pass in any formal sense to Parliament, and nearly two centuries after 1688 Queen Victoria was happily helping her relations on to the thrones of Europe and trying to undermine the authority of her ministers at home. But all that can be said of 1688, and it is quite a lot, is that from this time forward for better or worse the monarch recognized that death (or at least dishonor) would result if he and Parliament did part: *ultimate* (i.e., financial) power lay with Parliament. It was a long time before all foreigners realized this. Mrs. Simpson in the 1930s could still confuse the social influence of Lady Cunard and her set with real political power; to her consternation an indolent pipe-smoking ironmaster from the Midlands called Stanley Baldwin told her beloved Edward, King of England and Emperor of India, to abdicate from the throne and leave the country. As in 1688 only a handful of people, among them Winston Churchill, sided with the monarch, and on this occasion none joined him in his lonely exile. Churchill followed the example of his illustrious ancestor, John Churchill, Duke of Marlborough, by winning renown under the exile's successors.

The seventeenth century is easily the most exciting in modern English constitutional history: by comparison the eighteenth, which was to be so dramatic for the fortunes of America, domestically speaking at least is comparatively dull. The third period of English constitutional history starts about 1688 and ends with World War I. It saw the consolidation of the power of Parliament exercised through the Cabinet, though even towards the end of the period Edward VII was able to conduct a number of personal diplomatic negotiations on behalf of his government. By and large the monarch ceased to exercise the executive functions of government, let alone be the all-powerful sovereign of Elizabeth's day. Instead there was what constitutional authorities euphemistically called "the Crown"—power wielded apparently by the monarch but in fact by the Cabinet. It would also seem as though the British, far from wishing to publicize their democracy and freedom, tried to conceal what changes did occur in this direction, pretending all the while that what a nineteenth-century commentator, Walter Bagehot, called the dignified parts of government (especially the monarchy) were in fact efficient also.[4]

Towards the end of the period from 1688 to 1914, a conflict arose within Parliament itself owing to the extension of the franchise and the rise of modern political parties. Having joined forces to destroy the pretensions of the monarchy, the House of Lords and House of Commons became locked in deadly combat, the result being two elections in one year (1910) and the Parliament Act of 1911. By means of this Act the House of Commons established its supremacy, a supremacy made complete by the new Parliament Act of 1949. And so by 1914, confident that unlike most foreigners they were a free people who had nothing to fear from either monarch or nobility, Englishmen could go to the aid of "little Belgium." With President Wilson they fought the war to make the world safe for democracy (and the British Empire), merely adding the sensible footnote that with the coming of peace the nation should provide "homes fit for heroes." As often happens when wars are won, those heroes who did survive were on the whole left to fend for themselves. But if during the interwar period of 1919–1939 they did not elect Governments which could transform the country with the speed which had been possible between 1914 and 1918 they could only blame themselves. For by now the constitutional battles were for the most part over, and the all-powerful House of Commons was elected, after 1928, by universal suffrage.

It is still too early to describe at all accurately the era since 1918. Americans can divide the period 1919–1941 into the pallid normalcy of the 1920s and the Roosevelt roar of the New Deal in the 1930s, with the Depression looming in the background. To the British the whole interwar period has an aura of dismal disunity, of broken promises, unfulfilled hopes, of aimless direction

---

[4] The House of Commons, which exercises supreme financial power, still prefaces its grants of supply with the preamble, "We, Your Majesty's most dutiful and loyal subjects, the Commons of the United Kingdom and Parliament assembled . . ." But the real significance of this phrase, however, is that there is no mention of "the Lords Spiritual and Temporal" as in other legislation.

of affairs. The picture is of course overdrawn. The British middle classes probably suffered less than middle-class Americans. Instead there were black spots known as depressed areas and the nation's conscience was aroused over them as it had been over the issue of slavery a century or more earlier. But a considerable amount of development took place in the 1920s and 1930s—road construction, housing estates, light industries, and cinemas.

Table 1.4.   Parliamentary Reforms

Extension of franchise to:	
the middle class	1832
the working class	1867
agricultural laborers	1884
married women and spinsters over 30	1918
all women over 21	1928
Length of Parliament fixed at:	
three years	1694
seven years	1715
five years	1911
House of Lords reform:	
Powers reduced	1911
further reduced	1949
Composition altered:	
Life peers (law lords)	1876
Life peers (including women)	1958
Peerages renouncable	1963
Responsibility of Ministers (approx.):	
To the monarch	until 1714
To monarch and Parliament	1714–1841
To Parliament	1841–1868
To Parliament and electorate	1868–1911
To House of Commons and electorate	1911– —
Increasingly to Prime Minister	1940– —

One thing has become clear, at least since the Depression: the slow re-creation of the two-party system, and the Labour party's ouster of the Liberals. But the House of Commons has not been allowed to enjoy the fruits of its 1911 victory over the House of Lords. In its turn it has become virtually the junior partner in a political system dominated by the Cabinet, and, some would say, by the Prime Minister. In a sense the wheel has come full circle: once more power lies with "the Crown." Presumably now that "the Crown" consists of ministers, each of whom (except for those who are Lords) is elected by the people of a constituency, one can say that in a sense the people are supreme.[5] Government in Britain, like government in the United States (although in a very different way) is responsible to the people. Britain *is* a democracy.

A bird's-eye view of British constitutional history cannot fail to be an oversimplification, and it may even appear to be a confusing caricature. But at the risk of both, let us summarize what happened. Instead of a revolution providing a clear dividing line between the *ancien régime* and modern democracy, as in the United States, there was a long period of evolution. Many English people consider a few dates—1066, 1215, 1688, and 1832 in particular—to be milestones on the road to the liberty they now enjoy (and always did enjoy, so they will proudly and paradoxically boast). But it makes more sense to think of the country as ruled by the monarch so long as it was England alone which was being governed, i.e., from 1066 to 1603. With the accession of a Scots King in 1603 and the replacement of the Welsh Tudors by the Stuarts, a second phase in Britain's constitutional development occurred, one of struggle lasting from 1603 to 1688 between King and Parliament, Parliament being victorious. The third phase from 1688 to 1914 saw the evolution of the power of Parliament and finally the defeat of the Lords by the Commons. The fourth phase has seen the entrenchment of the power of the Government.

Thus today, just as the term "presidential government" is used to describe the American system (not Woodrow Wilson's "congressional government"), so the British speak of "cabinet government" instead of "parliamentary government."

This whole account of Britain's evolution may seem puzzling. Why has the nation which produced the Mother of Parliaments been so passive about democracy? Part of the answer is contained

---

[5] This was demonstrated in February, 1965 when the Foreign Secretary had to resign after being defeated in the general election and in a by-election.

in the question. As the creators of parliamentary government, the British have always felt that they were free in a way in which many peoples on the Continent were not. Their Parliament may not have been "democratic" in the modern sense of representing a cross-section of the population, but it was considered to represent the people in a very real sense when the King tried to extend the executive power. When addressing himself to the revolutionaries in France Edmund Burke, like Winston Churchill, felt able to speak with complete confidence on behalf of "the people of England."

But there is another explanation equally important. The English people have never really distinguished the freedom of the individual to determine his form of government from the freedom of the English people against foreign invasion. The great events of English history since 1215 concern foreign affairs as well as domestic. 1588 saw the defeat of the Spanish Armada and an attempt to conquer England. Marborough's wars, leading to the Peace of Utrecht of 1713, ended the threat of French domination until the rise of Napoleon and his defeat at sea in 1805 at Trafalgar and on land at Waterloo in 1815. Twice in the present century Britain has been threatened again, first in 1914 and again in 1940. She was saved by the Battle of the Marne in 1914 and the Battle of Britain in 1940 and survived to see the defeat of Hitler as well as the Kaiser. (The British are well aware that the Americans entered both wars reluctantly, suffered less and gained more—as the British did in earlier wars.)

English history books do not, therefore, use domestic events to mark off one era from another, unless they are old-fashioned enough to consider history to be divided by Tudors (1485–1603), Stuarts (1603–1714), and Hanoverians (1714 to the present). (Shakespeare lived in the reigns of both Elizabeth I and James I.) The three great periods of modern European history are the Peace of Utrecht (1713) to the Congress of Vienna (1815), 1815 to 1914, and 1914 to the present. In British textbooks the theme through all these periods, and the earlier ones, is the greatness of Britain and its resistance to foreign tyranny. Although the academic observer from afar may point out that the British have usually left the extension of their liberties to the upper and middle classes, the average Englishman is more conscious of the fact that (so he believes) he has lived in a country which has been free for 900 years. Whether he is right or wrong depends on whether one accepts the American idea of freedom or the British. Americans are perhaps justified in taking the British to task, for after all if the English people had not been so complacent in the eighteenth century the American Revolution might not have been necessary (or successful). On the other hand it is perhaps fair to try to see another country through the eyes of its people. Britain is and always will be a mystery and a paradox, the castle of conservatism and the cradle of parliamentary government. She has certainly experienced a most involved evolution, adopting pluralism while retaining her organic structure.

The Social Hierarchy

A hundred years ago Walter Bagehot in his classic *The English Constitution* described Britain as a deferential society. Today the expression is still used, particularly by foreigners, and usually in uncomplimentary terms. There are still traces of the Two Englands which Disraeli described in his novels, unfashionable though it is to say so in the light of all the statistics showing a more equitable distribution of the national income. The public opinion polls demonstrate the class basis of British politics clearly.

One must not be too hard on the English. Other European countries possess a social structure similarly if not more stratified, and in all of them the forces encouraging social mobility are very powerful. Upward mobility is a fact no less apparent in Europe than in North America; what remains is an institutional framework which seems more reactionary than it really is. The British upper classes have been remarkably quick to accept aggressive and successful self-made men; indeed that has been the key to the survival of the system. (It was a monumental blunder not to have given George Washington the British army regular commission that he so much coveted.) Because Britain's institutions, including

Table 1.5. Voting and Socioeconomic Class, 1945, 1950, 1959

% Sample 1959	Socioeconomic Class	% Conservative			% Labour		
		1945	1950	1959	1945	1950	1959
4	Average +	76	79	79	14	9	15
21	Average	61.5	68	66	22	15	14
62	Average −	} 30.5	35.5	34	} 54	53.5	46
13	Very poor		24.5	19		64	51

SOURCE: British Institute of Public Opinion.

the class system, have provided an element of stability, continuity, integrity, and even mystery, all of which stand in contrast to the rapid changes in the industrial world (where today's giant firm or trade union is tomorrow's sick man to be rescued by subvention or featherbedding), they have retained the respect of the man in the street. The English are deferential because they think they have much to be deferential about; and that to defer to those whom they think are superior, particularly in breeding, is not to fawn or to be subservient. The "gentleman" ideal has persisted because successful men have learned to behave like gentlemen. And there is no doubt that the British, at least until recently, have been fierce and ardent believers in the superiority of their way of life over the American.

In Britain, as in all countries, there is a difference in the style of life between the countryside and the cities. But nothing is more remarkable in England than the persistence of the old "feudal" (for want of a better word) traditions of behavior in many parts of the countryside. It is feudal in the sense that the traditional social structure is taken for granted and no one queries the right of "the gentry" to act as justices of the peace and to sit in Parliament as Conservative MPs. By contrast the United States' rural areas with their "courthouse rings" controlling the political machinery and the big business interests looming in the shadows behind them seem very much a "bourgeois" (again for want of a better term) society.

Nor is English Society confined to the countryside: it has set the tone of life in England generally. Despite its early and far-reaching industrialization, England remained a country dominated socially by an upper class which had its base in the countryside. For such a dispersed class to retain its sense of identity, private boarding schools have proved necessary. The English private system of education has been superb: but the reverse side of the coin has been a superiority and an inferiority complex on the part of those who have and those who do not have its advantages. Although England is _politically_ a democracy, it is arguable that the class distinction which to some extent it shares with other European countries has prevented it from being a *social* democracy in the North American sense.

Sources of Tension

It is often said, especially in England, that the United States is less conscious of class differences because it has been so pre-occupied with the problems of ethnic and racial tensions. But we should not assume too readily that Britain's problems are solely those of class. National sentiment and religious bigotry have played a part. There was for a long time a nationalist struggle carried on between England and the nations of the British Isles in the sphere of what today would be called ideology. But instead of the Communist doctrine which the Russians have used to dominate other nations in the Soviet bloc, there has been the much less widely known, but at times the very powerful, influence of the established church, particularly the Church of England. The Scots were among the first to have their own brand of Protestantism (as well as their own monarchy) and the Church of Scotland was established in 1560. The Welsh were not able to secure the disestablishment of the Church of England, which is now called The Church in Wales, until the Parliament Act had curbed the (Anglican) House of Lords in 1914. The Welsh orator, David Lloyd George, had become a powerful minister in the Liberal Government by that time. Meanwhile the Welsh, including Lloyd George himself, had long been Nonconformists. The very term *Nonconformist* contains a wealth of significance: whereas the American nonconformist tends to be an academic radical, an individualist perhaps with left wing political associations, the British Nonconformist has been a religious and perhaps nationalist radical who may be socially and politically conservative—like many nineteenth-century Wesleyan Methodists.

Nowhere was resistance to the Church of England greater than in Southern Ireland, which unlike Scotland, was Roman Catholic and subjugated. The English created bishoprics and

Anglican universities and the most famous university in Ireland remains the Protestant Trinity College, Dublin (now with a Catholic Chancellor), which nurtured Edmund Burke amongst other famous Irishmen.

Even in England itself opposition to the Church for centuries carried disabilities. Catholics were not emancipated until 1829 and Nonconformists could not graduate from Oxford and Cambridge until 1871. Only in the last century has religious freedom on the American pattern been a reality—and there is still the thorny question of the Anglican church's establishment (which provided the fashionable term of the 1950s to describe those in authority). Religious strife has been treated by some historians as a thing in itself but the establishment of the Church of England may have been in part the vehicle for the perhaps unconscious display of ethnic superiority by the English.

The old Catholics of ancient lineage are few in number; the British upper classes are overwhelmingly Protestant. It is true that there has been a decline in religious fervor, and it seems to have paralleled a decline in nationalism. But the decline of the Church of England may however merely signify a decline in English power, arrogance, and even self-confidence; and it could presage a new era of nationalism in the Celtic fringe no longer disguised as religion, whether Scottish Presbyterianism, Welsh Calvinism, or Irish Catholicism.

There are some observers who discern another source of tension in England: the million non-Caucasian immigrants, half from the West Indies and a third from India and Pakistan. Although less than 2 percent of the population, the Negroes and Asians are concentrated in certain sections of the larger cities and the relations between them and their white neighbors are not noticeably better than those in American cities. It is becoming increasingly difficult for the British (who never allowed foreign criticism of their colonial policies to cause them to be sceptical of the virtues of British democracy) to accuse the Americans of failing to practice the principles they preach. Racial tensions having thus been added to ethnic tensions, the British Isles now display some of the characteristics of the United States. In both instances differences in behavior are due for the most part to the disparity in the numbers involved and to history, not to any innate difference in national character.

Nevertheless religious and ethnic tensions have proved less pervasive than the sense of social status. Until recently the notion of a single supreme social hierarchy has mesmerized the British and has made the task of the Labour party doubly difficult. There has always been the temptation to accept honors (there are several trade union knights and lords) and invitations to aristocratic homes or the palace. Some have put up a stormy resistance to these blandishments, often offered in good faith but sometimes part of the deadly upper-class ploy known as the "aristocratic embrace," and the Labour party has been torn between radicals and conservatives in a manner impossible in a republic. There is on the one hand a feeling of class hostility, envy and resentment, and on the other a desperate desire to be accepted by Society.

There have been indications of a new American-style middle-class spirit emerging in Britain to replace the lower-class servility and the upper-class arrogance. The Labour party's first Prime Minister was an illegitimate child of the proletariat, J. R. Mac-Donald, himself seduced by the Conservative party in the early 1930s when he became leader of a so-called National Government which it dominated.[6] He was succeeded by two products of the best public schools—Attlee and Gaitskell. With the arrival of Harold Wilson on the scene in 1964, the middle class without a cultured accent had its spokesman, and not surprisingly he addressed himself to the middle-class scientists and technologists, two groups vital to the nation's survival but without the status afforded to their counterparts in North America.

The Role of the Mass Media

No description of British society would be complete without reference to mass media—the press, radio, and TV. Most Amer-

[6] On being invited by King George V to form a National Government in 1931 he is reported to have exclaimed: "Yes, tomorrow every Duchess in London will be wanting to kiss me."

ican newspapers are local in character, whereas by and large the British press is London-based. One or two national papers publish simultaneously in Manchester and Glasgow and so the Britisher, whether English, Scots, Welsh, or Irish can read a national morning paper at breakfast or on the way to work. (More people take a daily newspaper in Britain than in the United States, 506 per 1000 compared to 326.) This means that there is a unity of national opinion which demonstrates itself clearly at election time. The "swing" from one party to the other is usually pretty uniform from Lands End to John O'Groats, ranging from 1.4 percent in East Anglia to 4.4 percent in Scotland in 1964.

There is also a contrast in the quality of the newspapers. British newspapers tend to be sharply divided into the "posh papers"—*The Times, The Guardian, The Daily Telegraph,* and their Sunday equivalent, *Sunday Times* (quite separate from *The Times*), *The Observer,* and *Sunday Telegraph;* and the popular papers—*Daily Mail, Daily Express, Daily Mirror* with their Sunday counterparts.

In radio and television the British have tended to follow the European pattern of public ownership. At first—as in Canada, Sweden, and many other countries—radio was placed under a public corporation which could ensure that middle-class—and rather puritan middle-class—values (e.g., a daily service and nothing more vulgar than "light" music on Sundays) should be preserved. TV began in Britain in 1936 (before the U.S.), and was placed under the same auspices. Not until the 1950s and the pressures of some powerful advertising men, did commercial TV become a reality. Even so, advertisers are fairly rigorously controlled and do not sponsor actual programmes.

TV in Britain has tended to diminish the preponderance of London. There are many programmes from outside Britain, mostly from the U.S., and several networks are based outside London and try to emphasize their regional character. Formerly the BBC was a trifle stuffy (before the war even radio announcers after 6 P.M. wore dinner jackets to give the proper tone) but hidden persuaders on commercial TV have introduced much of the liveliness of American and Continental advertisers. Not all of it comes through the clipped British accent, but enough to

Table 1.6. Main National Daily Newspapers

Date Founded	Title	General Political Tendency	Circulation Average Jan.–June, 1965
1785	The Times	Independent	257,922
1821	The Guardian	Independent	275,900
1855	The Daily Telegraph	Conservative	1,350,529
1896	Daily Mail	Independent	2,424,810
1900	Daily Express	Independent	4,041,883
1903	Daily Mirror	Left of center	4,956,997
1909	Daily Sketch	Conservative	826,440
1964	The Sun	Left of center	1,361,090

SOURCE: *Britain: An Official Handbook, 1966*, London: Her Majesty's Stationery Office, 1966, p. 494.

assist in breaking down that provincialism which made it seem possible that the country would exchange the grandeur of imperialism and world responsibilities for the quiet stagnation of suburbia.

A Dependent Economy

England has not always been an overpopulated island dependent on the import of food and raw materials from distant ports of the globe. Until the industrial revolution her green and pleasant land provided an ample livelihood for her people: English roast beef was a byword and English woollens as treasured for their quality as they are today. English traders brought valuable cargoes from the East, and later from the West, and many of the great houses and parks of Britain are monuments to money that was made overseas. Three hundred years of empire were to leave an ample national legacy in property, houses, furniture, and investments which has not yet been squandered. The Hudson's Bay Company, founded in 1670 and now among other things owner of department stores in Canadian cities, still had its headquarters in London in 1965.

Yet the worldwide commercial success of England may have distorted her society, contributing to that divorce of the upper and lower classes which is found in many commercial economies. Industrialization and the setting up of small factories is a levelling influence which helps to explain the difference in social structure between, say Manchester and Liverpool, Pittsburgh and Boston, or Toronto and Montreal. Many of the interesting inequalities of British life predate the industrial revolution: it is even arguable that the passing of small-scale industry and the relative decline of the formerly sturdily independent North and Midlands have increased inequality and conformity. The great days of the Nonconformists, like those of the Liberal party, ended with World War I. Today the growth of large organizations, often influenced by American ideas and practices, is creating a society more like that of the United States.

The commercial expansion from the seventeenth century onwards and the industrial revolution which started in the eighteenth led to the strains of the nineteenth century when the population increased enormously and salvation was obtained not by war but by emigration to the United States and the dominions. Many of the people who went abroad were the most vigorous members of middle- and lower-middle-class society and their departure did nothing to bridge the gulf between Disraeli's Two Englands. Britain herself became increasingly dependent on these outlying dominions and later on the African and Indian empires which she conquered but did not always colonize. She could afford to forget the United States and the competition from Germany and to concentrate on her own protected markets. The Commonwealth and Empire received British capital and manufactured goods: in return they sent food and raw materials.

Two world wars radically altered this relationship. The Commonwealth countries recognized the unwisdom of depending for manufactures on a country which for a quarter of the period 1914–1945 was at war and unable to supply what was needed for their development. Instead they set about their own industrialization. Britain for her part doubted the wisdom of relying on distant countries for food and began an intensive programme of domestic agriculture. This has proved expensive, so expensive that two-thirds of the farmers' income is derived from government subventions. A few years ago it was discovered that the government spent more on subsidizing egg production than on universities.

But if the rest of the Commonwealth is no longer so dependent on Britain, Britain herself remains a dependent economy. She is unable to produce more than half of her food and she relies on imported raw materials for her industries. Coal has been mined in England for centuries, but modern factories and automobiles make the country increasingly dependent on oil, imported from the Middle East. Eighty-four percent of the power consumed in 1957 was from coal: five years later under 70 percent, and in 1965 65 percent, was from coal.

To pay for all these essentials Britain must export chemicals, textiles, cars, and aircraft. She must invent, manufacture, and above all sell the most intricate products of modern technology from aircraft engines to computers, and if she fails to produce sufficient inventors and designers, skilled workmen and entrepreneurs, and above all if she fails to outsell her American, German, and Japanese competitors, then she cannot purchase foreign goods and her standard of living will deteriorate. Nowadays most advanced economies are rapidly expanding and no *absolute* decline occurs anywhere in the West. But Britain's expansion has been sufficiently sluggish to cause alarm and there have been several sterling crises since 1945.[7] This means that from time to time foreign investors lose confidence in Britain and withdraw their funds from London. The British economy is on the horns of a dilemma: if it expands rapidly there is inflation, loss of confidence in the pound, and a weakening of Britain's *international* position: if official controls curb expansion the standard of living is kept low by government action and the *national* economy suffers. This ultimately also weakens the pound.

What has made the British people exceptional in the last few years is the tolerance with which they have viewed the re-emergence of their competitors, the decency with which they have relinquished their colonies, and their insistence on defending civilized values in a world constantly challenged by "materialism" whether this be Communist and dialectical or North American and economic. Few observers can see Britain regaining or even retaining her economic position in the world: yet few can fail to admire the spirit with which this people have met and surmounted their political problems. They have demonstrated a capacity to be good losers, even if this is a world which treats harshly those people who do not win.

---

[7] In real terms, the increase over the ten-year period to 1964 amounted to 30 percent.

CHAPTER TWO

Six Un-American
Principles of Government

HAVING PERSEVERED with the necessarily general social survey of an introductory chapter, the student of British government naturally wants to know what are the salient characteristics of the political system. Traditionally at this point attention is turned to the formal structure—Crown, Lords, and Commons. In many recent works this is preceded by an examination of the political process, of elections, parties and pressure groups.

But neither the structure of government nor the political process is of paramount importance to the American student of a foreign government. His first question, which we have already tried to answer is: How different is British society from American? His second, to be answered in this chapter, is: What are the principles underlying the British system? Having been taught the underlying assumptions of American government, he is tempted to assume that these are the bases of all democratic political systems. It may then come as a surprise to discover that underlying British government are six quite un-American principles. And since the British claim to be liberal-democrats it is worth examining what these are. For they are more important than, say, the number of standing committees in the House of Commons or the organizational structure of the Labour party.

The principles can be stated schematically.

The American principles are obvious enough and can be found in many a standard textbook. But the British principles of government are by no means agreed; it is even arguable that there are really no principles at all and that the system is primarily the consequence of custom and convention. In other words, according to this view, instead of explicitly enunciating principles like the American Founding Fathers, the British have merely inherited, and have occasionally modified, the practices of their forefathers.

Table 2.1.   Principles of Government

Six American Principles	Six Un-American Principles
1. A federalist structure	1. A unitary structure
2. Judicial review	2. Parliamentary sovereignty
3. Limited government	3. No written constitution
4. Separation of powers	4. The concept of the Crown
5. Checks and balances	5. Collective responsibility of the Cabinet
6. Popular sovereignty	6. A pluralistic but organic political system

Now if by principles we mean a narrowly defined set of political assumptions set out in a constitutional document, then this argument is valid: the British have few comparable principles. The great Victorian constitutional lawyer Dicey simply divided his *Law of the Constitution* into three sections:

I. The Sovereignty of Parliament
II. The Rule of Law
III. The Connection between the Law of the Constitution and the Conventions of the Constitution.

But if by principles we mean more than those explicitly laid down in a constitution; if instead we mean those basic assumptions of a constitution, sometimes stated but always implied; then the British have their principles as much as the Americans. Myrdal has said that

... America, compared to every other country in Western civilization, large or small, has the *most explicitly expressed* system of general ideas in reference to human relations. ... The American Creed is not merely . . . the implicit background of the nation's political and judicial order as it functions . . . the Creed has been made conscious to everyone in American society.[1]

By contrast, in Britain each commentator has to make his own selection of rules and practices which he may consider to be of "constitutional" importance.

It is because of the vagueness of the boundary between principles (which people believe in) and customs (which people take for granted) that authorities vary so much as they do. One of Dicey's modern critics, Sir Ivor Jennings, has listed four main principles of British government: "The British Constitution is democratic; it is parliamentary; it is monarchical; and it is a Cabinet system." Yet even this is unsatisfactory to the American student of government embarking on a comparative analysis.

A Unitary Structure

The traditional unitary structure of the British political system might seem to be a custom rather than a principle. This is not so. Although the English permitted federalism in the dominions, starting with Canada in 1867, they very definitely upheld unitary government in the British Isles. The cost has been very high, leading to rebellion and then the independence of the greater part of Ireland. Had federalism been adopted, the British Isles could have been divided into at least five provinces with more or less equal status: England, Scotland, Wales, Northern Ireland, and Southern Ireland. More sensibly, England itself would have been subdivided into four or five regions. The complex situation which instead prevails can be summarized in Table 2.2.

In addition, the unconquered Scots retain their separate legal system as well as their own established (Presbyterian) church. By contrast only the occasional use of its own language and the disestablishment of the Church of England, achieved 632 years after its conquest by the English, marks Wales off from England. It still has no agreed national capital.

[1] Author's italics.

Table 2.2. Political Structure of the British Isles

	Complete Independence	Own Parliament	Own Cabinet	Own Govt. Depts. and Local Govt. System	Own Minister
Irish Republic	Yes	Yes	Yes	Yes	—
Northern Ireland	No	Yes [a]	Yes	Yes	—
Scotland	No	No	No	Yes	Yes
Wales	No	No	No	No	Yes

[a] Northern Ireland also sends MPs to the Westminster House of Commons.

The Act of Union of England with Wales in 1536 effectively anglicized Wales and placed it under English jurisdiction. The Union with Scotland was quite different, beginning in 1603 with a union of Crowns. Though James I had trouble with his English Parliament he was able to dominate the Scottish Parliament by the device of committing its authority to a body nominated by the Crown and known as the Lords of the Articles. The Scots were defeated in the Civil War and conquered by Cromwell. In 1689 the Lords of the Articles were abolished. William III and Anne were unable to deal with the Scottish Estates as successfully as the Stuarts and there had to be either a separation of Crowns or a union of Parliaments. In 1707 the Act of Union was agreed to and the term Great Britain, invented by James I (and VI), henceforth had legal significance. The Union with Ireland in 1800 was a union of Parliaments alone, and this partly explains why the Irish, unlike the Scots or Welsh, agitated so fiercely for their own legislature, and in particular for home rule. The refusal to meet Irish demands led to rebellion and the break-up of the United Kingdom.

It would seem clear that whether the English admit it or not they have fought vigorously to uphold a unitary state at all costs. In doing so they have used the argument of the need for the supremacy of Parliament.

Parliamentary Sovereignty

No court of law can override the British Parliament: it is supreme. Judicial review is unknown. The principle of parliamentary sovereignty, now sometimes criticized as out-of-date, is one of the most treasured in British constitutional history. It signifies the glorious liberation of the people from royal tyranny. Thanks to the Civil War, power passed from the monarch to Parliament—not, be it noted, to "the people." As Blackstone put it, "When Parliament acts, every Englishman is intended to be there present either in person or by procuration and attorneys." In *Mein Kampf* Adolf Hitler compared the feeble legislature which met in Vienna in the final crumbling days of the Austro-Hungarian Empire when he was a youth with the prestige of the Parliament at Westminster, "the temple of the nation's glory." English schoolboys are brought up to admire those members of Parliament who opposed the Stuarts, such as Pym and Hampden, who fought the King rather than submit to arbitrary power.

Americans, naturally, are perturbed at the notion of any political institution, whether President or Congress, having supreme power, and viewed in the light of the experience of the American colonies (or the Irish Catholics) they have reason to prefer the check provided by judicial review. But it is important to realize that British experience is very different from the American. The eighteenth century with its troubles in India and North America —far-away places—and the argument over the separation of powers had far less influence on the constitutional tradition in Britain than the struggles of the seventeenth century which established the right of Parliament to curb the Crown.[2] Students of political theory cannot fail to notice the difference between the passionate turbulence of the age of Hobbes and Locke and the quietism which followed, relieved by the rational common sense of Hume and Bentham. Passion then became the prerogative of Americans (and Tom Paine) and of Frenchmen like Rousseau who scornfully observed that the British *thought* they were free because they had elections—a remark which, like many remarks made in the American colonies, were airily ignored in Britain itself where there was the widespread assumption that the *main* battle of King versus the people (i.e., the House of Commons) had been won a century earlier.

Of course in law the Queen-in-Parliament is not a single institution and legally the sovereignty of Parliament means the sovereignty of Queen, Lords, and Commons. By convention Parliament has traditionally meant the two houses and usually

[2] Yet compare the Declaratory Act of 1766 which established Parliament's power over the American colonies. The Colonial Laws Validity Act of 1865, passed during the negotiations to create the Dominion of Canada (1867), declared only laws passed in the colonies repugnant to those of the British Parliament to be invalid. This applied to the Dominions until the Statute of Westminster (1931) and is still a vital factor in colonial legislation.

the House of Commons alone. Nowadays the supremacy of Parliament is a more controversial question. It may even mean that the Prime Minister can do what he pleases provided he has the support of the Cabinet and his party in the House of Commons. This in turn may depend on the willingness of the Opposition and public opinion to acquiesce in his policies. He is limited not by any fundamental law but by opposition to his policies, since there is no written constitution.

No Written Constitution

Of all the principles this would seem to be the one which can be considered merely an inherited custom, and one which could easily be abandoned. For the British have expected each of their dependent territories to have a written constitution. However, it is just possible that all other nations have adopted constitutions out of expediency, and that the British alone have refused on grounds of principle. When England was in revolutionary ferment in the 1650s a constitution of sorts, the Instrument of Government, was proposed but proved impossible to enforce owing to the refusal of even Cromwell's Parliaments to feel bound by a written document. D. L. Keir put the point very clearly when he described the England of 1660:

Thus ended the age of written constitutions, inaugurated by the Ten Propositions and ended by the Additional Petition and Advice which had aimed at limited monarchy or republicanism. Such political expedients as written constitutions embodying inviolable rights, restricting sovereignty, and separating the legislative and executive powers, were henceforth discredited, as were single-chamber legislatures, and direct parliamentary appointment to office. Others, like a united Parliament for the three countries, reform of the franchise and redistribution of seats, were delayed for nearly two centuries through their premature achievement by the sword. The rejection of republicanism at least had been complete and final. Whether parliamentary, democratic, theocratic, or military it had met only with failure. A nation profoundly monarchist, anti-democratic, anti-sectarian, and anti-military had preserved, amid the stresses under which successive governments collapsed, the abiding sense that it was to be governed only by an authority based on law and not force, operating by virtue of consent and co-operation, and grounded upon a graded diversity of privilege and duty. It was to be the business of restored monarchy to adapt itself to these fundamentals.[3]

The anticonstitutional temper of England after the Civil Wars and Interregnum was clearly very different from that of the United States after the Revolutionary War. Even today the most vital enactments, such as the Parliament Act of 1911 which reduced the powers of the House of Lords, are treated as little more than expressions of general consensus—which can be modified (as was the Parliament Act in 1949) as soon as that consensus has changed. (The 1931 Statute of Westminster, which recognized the independence of the dominions, is presumably an exception.)

Thus England, unlike the United States, has not felt a need to spell out for all time, and for the pecuniary benefit of lawyers, the principles of government in a single constitutional document. England's Constitution is not primarily a document distilling the abundant (in the United States at least) wisdom of an oppressed people, the inspired vision of revolutionaries and the common sense of contemporary politicians anxious to limit the sphere of government. It is a somewhat abstract and foggy notion which few people fully comprehend, but which most people dimly understand because of custom and convention. Like the common law and Topsy it just grows; to a nation of gardeners it appears like a venerable oak tree which has weathered many storms. Many important persons, good as well as bad, have been hanged from its branches; even more have sheltered under its foliage; occasionally the nation has rallied to defend it against attack. Yet the British are not consciously aware of—or bothered by—the inevitable complexity and even confusion of their system. Few of them know what Magna Carta, the Petition of Right, the Habeas Corpus Act, or the Bill of Rights actually said and fewer still go on pilgrimages to Runnymede. (Instead, they visit the Tower of London, England's Bastille, to see the Crown Jewels.)

[3] D. L. Keir, *Constitutional History of Modern Britain Since 1485*, 7th ed., London: A. and C. Black, 1964, p. 229.

It would of course be a mistake to assume that all constitutions are as rigid as the American or that the British Constitution is flexible simply because it has not been codified.

Table 2.3.   Constitutional Documents

1215	*Magna Carta*. Protection against arbitrary punishment.
1628	*Petition of Right*. Commons condemned forced loans, arbitrary imprisonment and compulsory billeting of troops.
1679	*Habeas Corpus Act*. Accused persons not to be kept indefinitely without trial.
1689	*Bill of Rights*. Monarch forbidden to suspend a law, to levy taxation, or to maintain an army without parliamentary consent.
1700	*Act of Settlement*. Monarch not allowed to remove judges without consent of Parliament.
1931	*Statute of Westminster*. Grant of legal independence to (white) dominions.

The Concept of the Crown

There are two characteristics inextricably linked in the concept of the Crown. First there is the notion of a monarch as Head of State; second, the assumption that there is in the Crown the source of power.

Only in countries where the royal family has successfully adapted to a changing world has the monarchical institution been retained. Although there was a republic in Britain from 1649 to 1660 the monarchy was restored to the general satisfaction of most people (so far as one can tell). Apart from a minor republican movement expressing a certain irritation over the widowed Queen Victoria's longevity (she and George III ruled for the unconscionable time of 124 years out of the 141 between 1760 and 1901) there has been no widespread republican movement in Britain. Informed people realize that misconduct by but one sovereign could cause the end of the monarchy, but so far as can at present be foreseen the monarch as Head of State is a basic assumption of British government. Its importance is indicated by the insistence up to 1933 that the Irish should swear an oath of allegiance to the Crown.

The notion of the monarch as formal Head of State is intimately bound up with another equally important assumption—the Crown as the source of power. Cabinet ministers derive their authority not from election but by appointment as ministers of the Crown. Many of their powers are exercised as Crown prerogatives. By no means all powers were transferred from the monarch to Parliament during the struggle between them; many remained and with the rise of cabinet government were transferred to the Prime Minister and his Cabinet. These still find the concept of Crown prerogative irresistibly convenient. The fusion of powers means that up to a hundred members of the legislature may also be members of the Government, a situation which runs counter to the American notion of the separation of powers.

There is still some uncertainty regarding the precise nature of the Crown. To the politically naive the Crown means the monarch; to students of government the sovereign or monarch is "the person on whom the Crown is constitutionally conferred, whereas the Crown (which represents not only the Sovereign but also the Government) is the symbol of supreme executive power. The Crown vests in the Queen but in general its functions are exercised by Ministers responsible to Parliament." But to members of the Commonwealth, including the republics, the Crown seems to be something else again—the symbol of free association between independent states as stated in the Declaration of London, 1949. No doubt for the republican members this is almost meaningless, but for the British the concept of the Crown is a basic principle and they have insisted on acceptance of the monarch as head of the Commonwealth.

Collective Responsibility of the Cabinet

There is a marked difference between the relation of the Cabinet to the Prime Minister and that of the American Cabinet to the President. Even though British Secretaries of State and other Cabinet ministers may be primarily concerned with departments, and even though they may at times not be fully informed (as in the Suez crisis), they remain collectively responsible for the government of the country and they have a duty either to agree with that policy or to resign. This means that a Prime Minister asks the advice of outsiders at his peril, since if he draws too far away from his colleagues he may find that he has lost them—or, more seriously, that they no longer have confidence in him. An American President may lose the confidence of his Cabinet without worrying too much so long as he has the support of Congress and the people. But a Prime Minister is forever dependent on the goodwill of his colleagues: if they desert him he cannot continue.[4]

The doctrine of collective responsibility does not mean that all decisions are taken by the Cabinet as a whole; or that the Prime Minister is, as used to be thought, merely chairman of a committee where he is first among equals. But it does still mean that a minister must resign if he is unwilling to share in the responsibility for Government actions. Executive responsibility is not vested in the Prime Minister as it is in the President of the United States, but in the Crown.

In some ways collective responsibility is the counterpart of the checks and balances of the American Constitution. Instead of formal checks on the power of the Prime Minister there is the informal influence of the Cabinet upon him—and the informal dependence of the Cabinet on the goodwill of Parliament. At a time when the British Prime Minister is increasingly said to wield presidential power, and when Parliament is thought to be less influential than Congress, it is important to remember that in the British context a crucial role is played by the Cabinet. No Senate advises on appointments or consents to treaties: the Cabinet alone can check the Prime Minister in his use of patronage or conduct of foreign policy. Collective responsibility

---

[4] Jennings insists that it would be unconstitutional (sic) for the Queen to allow the Premier to dissolve Parliament in order to override his colleagues.

presumes fair play and the observance of certain conventions, but there is no guarantee that a Cabinet can really stop a Prime Minister unless it is prepared to resign as a body.

A Pluralistic but Organic Political System

By contrast with other European countries where there has traditionally been a large amount of governmental control over national life (the Swedes, for example, have a ministry in charge of the Lutheran state church which is also responsible for education up to and including university level) the British, like the Americans, have always permitted countless semi-independent organizations to flourish and to exercise political influence. There are medical associations, trade unions, business organizations, universities, churches—the list is endless. It is amazing in a way that they all manage to live together in a state of mutual tolerance, and it is only because Anglo-Saxon society has for centuries operated in this haphazard fashion (having escaped the age of absolutism) that the system, if it is a system, works. Britain is a pluralistic society.

But it is pluralistic with a difference. Owing to the monarchical and imperial tradition the Government, representing the Crown, chooses which groups it will recognize and give, if it so wishes, consultative status. This means that all interest groups are not equal: some trade unions, some professional organizations, and some business associations are officially recognized and some are not. The system is therefore also organic in the traditional sense of the term. The Crown is head of the body politic and to some extent determines the policies of its members. A trade union is well advised to demonstrate that it has the solid backing of its members and has a responsible secretary. It will be treated not only as a pressure group but as a responsible adviser and the secretary may end his days with the accolade of a title. It is partly this informal system of official recognition that has led to the coinage of the term "Establishment" to cover all those groups and leaders who are (and feel) "in" with those in power.[5] It is probably a unique arrangement, although people in other countries profess to detect Establishments of their own.

There are many people who confuse this modern proliferating, pluralistic "Establishment" of business, professional, and trade union organizations with that smaller group of interests which have been traditionally established by law or prerogative—that is to say elements of an organic structure which not only enjoy governmental recognition but are directly or indirectly part of the machinery of government. The (established) Church of England is of course the prime example but there are many others. All government departments and agencies established or chartered by the Crown, e.g., the Forestry Commission, Atomic Energy Authority, the BBC, the universities, the nationalized industries and even older business firms established by royal charter, come into this category. There is a general understanding that to be part of the established order is to conform to a certain code of behavior. For example, the royal favor has been extended to many business firms which can proudly boast the sign "By Royal Appointment."

In all these expressions of an organic society which America has not known since 1776 there are no doubt relics of a feudal era when men of substance—and companies of men—hoped to obtain a coat of arms, to be recognized by the College of Heraldry, and to be bound to their sovereign by mutually satisfactory ties of rights and duties. This tenuous link with the past was almost broken by the industrial revolution and the growth of Nonconformity, a popular press, trade unions and the Labour party, but in the absence of a revolution the conservative elements in British society (at least until 1964) so successfully preserved their position that it was possible not only to describe a traditional Establishment but to discern the ramifications of the new pluralistic (or counter-) Establishment encompassing all aspects of British life. The monarchy persists, the House of Lords has

[5] Since 1937 there has existed an official Opposition in Parliament recognized by law. It is arguable that by this means the Labour party was brought into the Establishment.

survived several reforms, and even the House of Commons attends to its traditional ritual. In no sense is Britain really a liberal republic in all but name.

It would therefore be fair to consider Britain, like the United States, a pluralistic society. But this needs to be qualified lest the American principle of popular sovereignty be assumed also to be accepted. It is, rather, a pluralistic-organic political system. As the American scholar, A. L. Lowell observed many years ago, British government "has grown up by a continual series of adaptations. . . . In this it is like a living organism." [6]

[6] A. L. Lowell, The Government of England, New York: Macmillan, 1908, I, p. 14.

PART II

*Government
in Operation*

The most important element in British government is the Cabinet, and the Prime Minister in particular. By comparison the monarch, the Lords, and for much of the time even the House of Commons, are relatively minor figures.

This raises a peculiar problem. So long as Parliament was (or was thought to be) the center of the stage, with its debates not only published in Hansard but summarized in the leading newspapers, the nature of government policy was discernible. Whether this idyllic picture of British—or any other—government was ever accurate is open to question, but it is certainly not an adequate picture nowadays. There are parliamentary party meetings which are held in secret, there are pressure group activities behind the scenes, and there are great offices of state which despite Question Time in the House of Commons are largely shielded from public view. In the last analysis Government policy is determined in Cabinet meetings; it is precisely at this point, the key to the whole system, that least is known as to what goes on. Until the establishment of the Cabinet secretariat in 1916, often only the Prime Minister knew what had been decided.

It is true that there are government reports—White Papers and Blue Books. There are also biographies and statesmen's memoirs, including those of Winston Churchill, and no country has such a plethora (and, one might add, such a need) of these as Britain. But they are secondary sources, and even memoirs are the subjective impressions of men perhaps too close to events to have proper perspective. They are no substitute for an examination of Cabinet minutes, the briefs which departments present to the Cabinet, or the proposals which circulate in draft between departments and the Treasury before the budget is produced.

American politicians seem to have had fewer scruples about the secrets of the past. The provisions of the 1945 Yalta Agreements, and indeed the whole discussion, were published within ten years, much to the delight of scholars, foreign as well as

American. In its secrecy of operation British government stands somewhere between the Russian and the American. The House of Commons is as free and open as Congress and is very different from the Supreme Soviet. But the inner workings of government are more concealed from the public view than events in Washington, where prying things out has been less difficult than keeping things secret.

There are at least three reasons for this difference. The organic British political system enables the civil service elite, backed by the Cabinet, to rebuff the press and to blackball those of its members who break the code of reticence. An American leader seems always to be surrounded by a mass of photographers and reporters. In England, he would be protected as far as possible from what is called "the glare of publicity." For the organic tradition assumes that a leader wishes to avoid publicity, not because of modesty but because he is already sufficiently well known to those who make important decisions. It may be no accident that as the organic (and aristocratic) tradition has declined in England the desire to avoid publicity seems to have become less pronounced; today every Prime Minister has his public relations adviser.

Secondly, there is none of the separation of powers which in American government gives Congress a right to probe administration and even to cut the budget and harass civil servants. To defend themselves, American civil servants must explain their policy and secrecy may do a great deal of harm. In Britain civil servants are attacked only indirectly—through the minister, and it is he who must take the blame if they make mistakes, not they.

In the third place, there is the tradition of the sovereignty of the Crown. The notion of the sovereignty of the people means that the Americans think they have a right to know what is going on in their government. Americans are very much aware that the civil service is spending the taxpayers' money. By contrast demands for British income tax are mailed "On Her Majesty's Service," the Post Office carries the Royal Mail, and ministers, we must repeat, are ministers of the Crown. Even the Opposition in Parliament has only limited access to information. The British pride themselves on having a "loyal and responsible" Opposition. It must be difficult to act "responsibly" without access to official documents, and the Labour party did much better in the early years of postwar opposition (1951–1953) than later because it had had this access from 1945 to 1951.

CHAPTER THREE

The Prime Minister and His Cabinet: Quasi-Presidential Government?

> *Insofar as Ministers feel themselves to be agents of the Premier the British Cabinet has now come to resemble the American Cabinet.*
>
> R. H. S. Crossman

IF THE OPERATIONS of government are concealed in large measure from public view, what is the value of an attempt to describe British government? The answer to this is quite straightforward. Provided it is recognized that there are serious gaps in our knowledge, no harm (and much good) is done by examining those features which are open to public view. These are sufficiently numerous for some understanding of the difference in structure and operation between American and British government to be possible.

There seem to have been three stages in the modern evolution of British government. Until the middle of the nineteenth century, the first stage, the "government" was assumed to be the Crown, Lords, and Commons. From then until World War II it was assumed to refer to the ministry alone and the term cabinet government tended to replace parliamentary government (a distinction sometimes being drawn between the Government, i.e., Cabinet, and British government, i.e., the political system.)

Cabinet—or parliamentary—government is supposed to be distinguished from presidential government by the fact that the Government is individually and collectively "responsible," i.e., dependent on the goodwill of the legislature.

In recent years there has been a tendency to consider even the term cabinet government a misnomer, and to stress the role of the Prime Minister. For example, since 1918 the Prime Minister alone has recommended to the sovereign the dissolution of Parliament. The notion that the Cabinet's distinctive character is its sense of collective responsibility has been criticized; instead, so it is urged, the Prime Minister plays a quasi-presidential role with ministers feeling responsible for the conduct of their departments more to him than to the House of Commons. The failure of the modern House to pass a vote of censure on the Government or even to cause the dismissal of a minister suggests to some that collective responsibility is as out of date as impeachment is in both the United States and the United Kingdom. Ministers lose their jobs and their salaries because the Prime Minister dismisses them.

In this chapter we shall examine the role of the Prime Minister, outline the ministerial hierarchy, and consider the duties of ministers collectively in Cabinet and individually as heads of departments. Finally, we shall take a further look at the fashionable notion of quasi-presidential government.

The Role of the Prime Minister

The Prime Minister is selected by the sovereign. He (or she) chooses a man who can command the support of a majority of the members of the House of Commons. Such a man is normally the leader of the largest party in the House. Where two parties are rivals in a three-party contest such as those which occurred in the 1920s he is usually selected from the party which wins the greatest number of seats. The Prime Minister is assumed to be the choice of his party and nowadays, so far as can be ascertained, the monarch's part is a formality.

Anyone selected for the highest political office has to be a man of parts, though it has been suggested that he should be "an uncommon man of common opinions." Not all Prime Ministers seem to have been fitted for their task, but certainly all of them have had to pass one important test: the day-to-day scrutiny of their motives and behavior by fellow members of Parliament before they were ultimately elected to the leadership of their party. All Prime Ministers, unlike many Presidents, have served a long apprenticeship in the legislature and have been ministers in previous Cabinets.

It is at this point, when we ask the simple question: What are the statutory duties and responsibilities of the Prime Minister? that the conventional nature of British government becomes apparent. For whereas the duties of the President are laid down in the Constitution, the powers of the Prime Minister are almost nowhere spelled out in a statute. Unlike his fellow ministers he does not receive the seals of office: he merely kisses the hands of the monarch like an ambassador.

The Prime Minister has four main areas of responsibility. He is head of the Government; he speaks for the Government in the House of Commons; he is the link between the Government and the sovereign; and he is the leader of the nation. He is chief executive, chief legislator, and chief administrator.

As head of the Government the Prime Minister has the power to recommend the appointment and dismissal of all other ministers. Far from being merely first among equals, he is the dominant figure. Ministers wait in the hall of No. 10 Downing Street before being called into the Cabinet room. He may himself hold other portfolios such as that of Foreign Secretary (as did Lord Salisbury) or Minister of Defense (as did Mr. Churchill). He has general supervision over all departments and appoints both the Permanent Secretary (the senior civil servant) and the Parliamentary Secretary (the junior minister). The Cabinet Office keeps a record of Cabinet decisions and ensures that the Prime Minister has up to date information. He controls the agenda which the Office prepares for Cabinet meetings. There is a smaller Prime Minister's Private Office which consists of a principal private secretary and half a dozen other staff drawn from the civil service. Perhaps owing to American influence the two offices are becoming increasingly important and there are signs that the Prime Minister is no longer content to be aided by nonpolitical civil servants. There is little doubt that if he chooses (and if he is able) the Prime Minister can be in complete command of his Cabinet.

The Premier must also give leadership in the House of Commons, though he usually appoints a colleague as Leader of the House. He speaks for the Government on important matters—increasingly, questions are directed to him personally—and controls the business of the House through the Future Legislation Committee of the Cabinet which he appoints mainly from the senior nondepartmental ministers. Since the success of his legislative programme depends on the willing support of his party in the lobbies he must attend to his duties as party leader and ensure that the party machinery, both parliamentary and national, is in the hands of men he can trust. Though he alone can request the sovereign to dissolve Parliament and call a new election, it is open to debate whether it is this power that enables him to control his party and the House. But certainly the timing of an election is entirely in his hands—provided that Parliament does not exceed its five-year term and that he has a good majority.

As link between the Government and the sovereign the Prime Minister keeps the monarch cognisant of what is going on in Cabinet and in the world at large. It is easy to dismiss the monarch as politically impotent, but no one can deny that there are many occasions when by a careless word the monarch can damage the reputation of the Government and even the country. It is for the Prime Minister, through his weekly audience with the monarch, to ensure that he or she is well informed. Other ministers may approach the monarch only with his permission (though the monarch can see whomever he or she chooses).

A great many appointments have to be made by the Crown. Some are the prerogative of the monarch: some are part of the patronage of the Premier; most are "in the gift of the Crown" which means in practice the Premier. He can exercise much discretion (and occasionally, as in Mr. MacDonald's appointment of the Rev. Hewlett Johnson, destined to be known as the "Red Dean" of Canterbury, some indiscretion) in the appointment of judges, ecclesiastics, Regius professors and senior officers in the armed forces. He is responsible for the Honours List, advised by a Political Honours Scrutiny Committee.

Finally, the Prime Minister is leader of the nation. In time of crisis the people expect him to make an announcement and to appear on television. Increasingly he should be a man who can not only secure the confidence of the House of Commons but of the man in the street, or rather the TV viewer in the armchair. Elections are ostensibly fought between individual parliamentary candidates, but in practice they are contests between national parties which offer their own programmes (or panaceas). The parties convey an "image" to the nation through the voice and appearance of their leaders. The Prime Minister must outshine his rival, the Leader of the Opposition. In the 1964 election, when the Liberals doubled their vote, much importance was attached to the TV performance of the Liberal leader, Jo Grimond.

The Head of State and traditional "symbol of the Nation" may be the monarch, but the chief executive is in reality the Prime Minister. It is to his desk that ultimately all difficult problems come, whether these involve participation in NATO, the balance of payments crisis, the budget—or even the monarch's love affairs (as in 1936). It is the Prime Minister who symbolizes Britain's policies abroad and it is he who must personally convince political leaders in other countries that his Government can be relied upon.

The Prime Minister is also chief legislator. Through the Future Legislation Committee, he determines which bills the House of Commons will discuss during the session, and can attach whatever importance he chooses to the Immigration Bill or Steel Nationalization Bill. With few exceptions bills are introduced in the House by the Government and if they are important they require the backing of the Premier.

Also, he is chief administrator. Not only does he supervise the departments and chair Cabinet meetings but he directs the Cabinet Office and the Office of the Prime Minister. In economic affairs he decides governmental strategy in conjunction with his Chancellor of the Exchequer and Minister for Economic Affairs, if there is one, and leaves these ministers to implement his policies. In defense policy he chairs the Defense Committee of the Cabinet, leaving the details to the Secretary of Defense, the three Ministers for Defense (Army, Navy, and Air Force) and the Chiefs of Staff. Foreign Affairs, the immediate responsibility of the Foreign Secretary, require the intervention of the Prime Minister when policy is initiated and agreements finally concluded. This is not to suggest that the Prime Minister initiates policy in all fields, but rather that external events compel him to devote his energies to all of them. An examination of Mr. Wilson's "first hundred days" of office in the fall of 1964 shows that the balance of payments crisis compelled him to attend first to economic policy in October. Then the need to clarify Britain's role in NATO compelled a reappraisal of defense policy in November. Finally, the ground having been cleared by the Foreign Secretary, in December the Prime Minister consulted foreign Heads of Government and made clear the lines of his Government's foreign policy. (In practice things did not work out quite so neatly: the NATO reappraisal was interrupted by renewed pressure on the pound and the balance of payments crisis overshadowed everything else.)

As chief executive, chief legislator and chief administrator, the Prime Minister is potentially a very powerful individual. Everything depends on the use which he chooses to make of his position, and the success with which he delegates some of his responsibilities.

The Ministerial Hierarchy

At least 70 members of Parliament are invited to join the Government after an election. In 1964 the total number was 102 out of a Labour party of 317—or nearly a third. This is far too large a body ever to be gathered together conveniently in one place and a distinction is drawn between the various levels in the ministerial hierarchy, "ministers" being the generic term for all those who hold office.

At the top is the Prime Minister and below him is usually an inner circle and/or a group of senior ministers. The leading departmental ministers tend to be the Foreign Secretary, the Home Secretary, and the Chancellor of the Exchequer; but these may not compose the inner circle to whom the Prime Minister turns for advice when quick decisions have to be taken. In other words, it is unwise to identify senior ministers with the inner circle of any given Premier, though the two circles usually overlap. Below the Prime Minister, senior ministers and inner circle there is the rest of the Cabinet, which numbered 23 in all in November 1964 (see Table 3.1). The Cabinet is therefore composed as follows:

Prime Minister
Senior ministers: inner circle (about 3 to 6)
Remainder of Cabinet (15 or more)

Most ministers today do not even have a seat in the Cabinet. In November 1964, no less than 27 Ministers of Cabinet rank were outside the Cabinet, including the Postmaster General and Minister of Aviation. Fourteen of them were Ministers of State in important Departments whose heads were members of the Cabinet. At the bottom of the hierarchy were 52 junior ministers such as Parliamentary Secretaries. The hierarchy is completed with

Ministers of Cabinet rank outside the Cabinet, Ministers of State
Junior ministers, e.g., Parliamentary Secretaries

Traditionally a government department has had a minister in charge and a junior minister assisting his chief, often in the other house. The growth of departments has meant that some departments require two senior ministers or even more. In the Ministry of Defense, for example, there were seven ministers in November 1964.

Secretary for Defense (in the Cabinet)
Deputy Secretary for Defense and
   Minister of Defense for the Army
Minister of Defense for the Royal Navy
Minister of Defense for the Royal Air Force

} Ministers of Cabinet rank

3 Under Secretaries of State for Defense—junior ministers
There were no Ministers of State.

Table 3.1. The British Cabinet, November, 1964

---

[a] Prime Minister and First Lord of the Treasury
First Secretary of State and Minister for
   Economic Affairs
[a] Secretary of State for Foreign Affairs
[a] Lord President of the Council and Leader of
   the House of Commons
[a] Lord High Chancellor
[a] Chancellor of the Exchequer
[a] Secretary of State for the Home Department
[a] Secretary of State for Commonwealth Relations
[a] Secretary of State for Colonial Affairs
[a] President of the Board of Trade
Secretary of State for Education and Science
[a] Secretary of State for Defense
[a] Lord Privy Seal and Leader of the House of Lords
Chancellor of the Duchy of Lancaster
Minister of Agriculture, Fisheries and Food
Minister of Transport
[a] Minister of Labor
Minister of Housing and Local Government
Minister of Power
Minister of Technology
Minister of Overseas Development
[a] Secretary of State for Scotland
Secretary of State for Wales

---

[a] These ministers have been included in every Cabinet since 1945.

Table 3.2 indicates the normal road to power up the ministerial hierarchy. Many never reach the ministry: some start near the top. Thus Sir Charles (C. P.) Snow was appointed Parliamentary Secretary to the Ministry of Technology in October 1964 although he was not even an MP. (He was made a peer.)

On the whole the office of Secretary of State is senior to that of Minister. Some departments are permanent, but others are established, abolished and sometimes recreated with a slightly different title, rather like American agencies. A few offices seem permanently represented in the Cabinet but even this is deceptive. The Chief Secretary for Ireland once seemed a fixture: so until recently has seemed the Secretary for Colonial Affairs.

The Cabinet

In 1918, before the focus of interest was the Prime Minister, the Haldane Committee on the Machinery of Government stated that the Cabinet had three main functions:

1. the final determination of policy to be submitted to Parliament
2. the supreme control of the national executive in accordance with the policy prescribed by Parliament
3. the continuous coordination and delimitation of the activities of several Departments of State.

As we have seen, in a very real sense nowadays this responsibility is exercised by the Prime Minister. Ministers themselves are primarily concerned with the tasks which he allots them. Instead of the Cabinet being a talking shop it is a professionally organized group of administrators who function much like a university senate—via committees. And just as a university senate comprises persons who often have considerable administrative responsibilities, so members of the Cabinet are departmental administrators as well as part of the supreme policy-making executive.

The notion that the Cabinet ever approximated a debating society is somewhat far-fetched. It always was an organization to which matters were submitted only when there was disagreement between ministers, or when the Prime Minister was undecided, or when matters of state required the sounding out of opinion and the willingness of the Cabinet to take responsibility for unpleasant decisions.

Yet the phrase "Cabinet responsibility" is clearly meant to signify a particular way of conducting government. Traditionally the Cabinet has been considered to be a team which stands or falls by its collective policy, and to judge from many accounts Cabinet members have in the past at least thought of themselves in this light. But the Cabinet meets only once or twice a week for a couple of hours each time, hardly enough for adequate discussion of the nation's business in any detail.

Table 3.2. The Road to Ministerial Power

Prime Minister Inner Cabinet Cabinet minister	} Cabinet minister	} MINISTER
Minister of Cabinet rank Non-Cabinet minister, e.g., Minister of State Junior minister, e.g., Parliamentary Secretary or Under Secretary of State		
Parliamentary private secretary to a minister Member of Parliament	} BACKBENCHER	
Parliamentary candidate		

NOTE: Even those who proceed steadily upwards may expect to spend some time on the Opposition benches. *Britain: An Official Handbook, 1965* is less concerned with power and divides ministers into the following categories (pp. 45–46):

1. Prime Minister
2. Non-Departmental ministers
3. Departmental ministers
4. Lord Chancellor and law officers
5. Ministers of State
6. Junior ministers

It also says the Prime Minister is appointed by *the Crown*.

Individual Cabinet Ministers

Ministers have at least half a dozen responsibilities as individuals. Like other MPs, they have constituents to placate and they must be good party colleagues. Even more than backbenchers, however, they must defend party policy, keeping recalcitrant colleagues in line through their example, and they must be able to keep the respect, if not always the attention, of the House. But these three responsibilities—to constituents, to the party, and to the House—are all shared with fellow MPs.

Three other duties are borne by ministers alone. Above all, a departmental minister must attend to the business of his department. In theory he works in Whitehall in the morning and attends debates at Westminster in the afternoon and evening, taking time out for dinner. In practice he is often too busy to attend Parliament except when he is required to answer questions in the House or to take part in debates. Individually each minister is responsible to Parliament for his department and if a scandal occurs it is the minister who is constitutionally responsible and who may have to resign.

Another duty of a minister is to sit on Cabinet committees where so much of the coordination of Government business is done. Little is known about this aspect of government owing to the secrecy rule, but there can be little doubt that it is one of the reasons for ministers having less time to spend in the Commons.

Finally of course the minister has to attend Cabinet meetings twice a week. He may be a forceful contributor to the solution of the nation's problems or merely a good listener, pleased to be a participant in such high-level discussions. But he must always remember that however uninterested he may be in some of the issues raised, as a member of the Cabinet he is accountable to Parliament for whatever decisions are taken.

Cabinet or Quasi-Presidential Government?

There is so much loose talk about the decline of parliamentary and cabinet government and the rise of the presidential Prime Minister that it is worth examining the two systems to see whether by some mysterious alchemy parliamentary (including cabinet) government can be transformed—if not into presidential government then at least quasi-presidential government.

In a formal sense it obviously cannot. As we saw in Chapter Two the American presidential system is predicated on judicial review of the executive and legislature, not the sovereignty of Parliament; and on government strictly limited by statute, not loosely based on conventions. In practice British government could become more like American government if the conventions ceased to work—if, for example, Cabinet ministers began to act as advisers to the Premier; if policy was determined by the Premier rather than by collective action; if Parliament because of party discipline ceased to hold the executive responsible; if the Prime Minister claimed that he alone could exercise the Crown's prerogative of making treaties, declaring war, etc. There are indications that such changes are under way and that the power of the Prime Minister has been increasing, but so far there is no firm evidence that the basic assumption of cabinet government—its responsibility to the legislature—has been forgotten either by the Cabinet or by Parliament.

Yet there is a very real danger that the many difficulties which Britain has encountered may tempt a Prime Minister to take forceful action personally, action which some may consider unconstitutional. The parliamentary system assumes that the Prime Minister is a coordinator rather than an innovator, a chairman of committees rather than an independent director of policies in time of peace. In wartime the system has had to be modified and the question arises whether the British will ever enjoy the luxury of genuine peace again. Moreover, the decline of Britain may lead to a decay in that bold parliamentary spirit which kept the King's ministers in check over the centuries. The very nature of modern government with its complexity may make the presidential mode of operation (in the sense of a powerful Prime Minister willing to appoint as advisers people who are not MPs) the most practical one, particularly for the Labour party.

Why should this be so? British parliamentary government assumes that a great many capable men will be attracted to parliamentary service. This is still true for Conservatives who can combine politics with a business or professional career, but it is less easy for Labour supporters, many of whom must give up their jobs—and even future careers—entirely. Those re-elected in 1964 had spent up to thirteen years on the Opposition benches and several leading MPs had abandoned the struggle. There has been a certain unease about the effect of thirteen years in the "wilderness" on the caliber of Labour leaders and it was thought significant that when Mr. Wilson set up an important new ministry—Technology—he felt constrained to go outside Parliament for both its ministers. Once the road to the Cabinet ceases to lie for the most part through the House of Commons, that chamber, like the Lords, may no longer attract men who are able administrators as well as useful orators.

Should the trend towards presidential government continue it could have serious consequences because there are no formal checks and balances in the British Constitution. The hands of the judges have been tied since the parliamentary victories of the seventeenth century. The hands of the backbenchers have been tied by rigorous party discipline. All that remains is the willingness of the Cabinet to operate the political system as it has been intended to work. If the Cabinet were to fail in this responsibility—and some observers seem to think it has already failed—then the Prime Minister would have a much freer hand than the American President. Instead of exercising powers granted to him in the Constitution, he wields the massive "prerogatives of the Crown." No institution would be able to restrain him.

There would of course be one solution to this problem: a written Constitution limiting the powers of the executive. Unless the British adopted an American-style Constitution the system could never become presidential in the American sense, either in theory or in practice. For the emergence of a powerful Prime Minister would not mean a "presidential" system of government. It would be "quasi-presidential" government in which the Prime Minister had the power but not the legal limitations of an American President. It would be neither presidential nor parliamentary. Yet such a trend is possible if the country remains in a state of crisis and if the traditional network of power is unable to respond adequately, as in France in 1958 before De Gaulle came to power.

The acid test of a political system, it must be remembered, is not whether ministers are *supposed* to act collectively and responsibly—but whether they in fact do. So far at any rate, despite gloomy forebodings to the contrary, British Cabinet ministers have not failed in this important duty. Nor, it should be added, have MPs. A Prime Minister, unlike the President, still addresses Parliament before he speaks to the people on television, recognizing that parliamentary sovereignty, not popular sovereignty or the separation of powers, is an important principle of British government.

CHAPTER FOUR

The Half-Revolution:
Decision Making 1945-1965

THE BRITISH have long been admired for the way in which they have conducted their political affairs. But they have been under mounting criticism for their failure to develop a dynamic economy. It is becoming increasingly difficult to describe the British political system, especially now that it is the government which is responsible for social and economic policy, without considering its shortcomings. Ultimately all systems are judged as much by what they achieve as by the way they go about their business: by their capacity to produce economic growth as much as by their legislative procedures.

In this chapter we shall compare the intentions of British postwar Governments to promote prosperity with the realities of British life twenty years later. The Labour Government of 1945 was determined to avoid the mistakes following 1918, when high hopes were dashed and the interwar period 1919–1939 became notorious for the inability of Britain to regain her prewar economic and financial predominance in the world. In 1945 nationalization, socialized medicine, and government planning were intended to bring about a revolution in British economic and social policy— but not in financial policy, for it was obvious by then that the dollar had replaced the pound as the world's leading currency.

Britain proved to have the capacity for an *administrative* revolution, and much of her society and economy ranging from the Bank of England to the local gasworks was reorganized. But she lacked the capacity to make this formidable administrative reorganization of the late 1940s the foundation of a new and dynamic society and economy, the proud showpiece of democratic socialism for which the Labour party hoped. The reforms suggested that Britain, unlike Germany or Japan, had lost faith in capitalism without gaining confidence in a Communist-type direction of the whole economy—or even in the plan which the French later introduced.

And so, instead of an economic and social revolution, there was to be at best a half-revolution. Britain may have made the mistake of choosing as her ideal the so-called Middle Way.

Great Expectations: The 1940s

When the Labour party won the election of 1945 the stage was already set for a reform government. Unlike many other European empires the British Empire had remained intact after 1918, her only revolution being in Ireland. The monarchy remained unshaken and the Conservative party returned to power for most of the interwar period. There were strikes in the postwar years but in restrospect the main domestic legacy of this era was ultimately to be the bold decision of the Labour party to insert a clause in its 1918 constitution proclaiming the common ownership of the means of production, distribution, and exchange. Forty years later the party was to try vainly to rid itself of the albatross of Clause 4.

The Great Depression of 1929–1933 did not lead to any considerable Fascist movement. Nor was there a New Deal. Instead, blame for the crisis tended to be put on the Labour Government of 1929–1931. The 1930s, like the 1920s, saw a return to normalcy in the shape of the Conservatives, this time disguised as a National Government. But there were many intellectuals on the Left who were dissatisfied with the Government and through books and pamphlets prepared the way for the changes which occurred in the 1940s.

When war broke out in 1939 the British people were united

once again. A year later under Winston Churchill they narrowly defeated the German threat of invasion in what he called their finest hour. Soon there was enough energy and confidence not only to prosecute the war but to plan for the peace and a new Britain. Men in all parties were determined that the postwar era would justify the effort expended on the war. In late 1942 at the time of the Battles of Alamein and Stalingrad, Beveridge produced the *Report* which was to inspire the postwar system of social security. R. A. Butler saw his Education Act pass through the House of Commons in 1944, the year of the Normandy invasion.

The new Labour Cabinet of 1945 did more than implement the proposals of the wartime coalition under Churchill to improve the health, housing, and education of the people. It refurbished a number of prewar government reports on the need to "rationalize" certain basic industries and utilities by reducing the number of small firms in operation, and remembering its promise of 1918 set about their *nationalization* with considerable vigor through the creation of state-owned monopolies. By common agreement the coal mines were nationalized in 1946, and by 1949 virtually all the nationalization acts had been passed, thousands of private and municipal undertakings being absorbed into giant state monopolies. As if to celebrate the transformation of the country, one of the last acts of the Labour Government of 1945–1951 was to promote the Festival of Britain, a century after the Great Exhibition of Queen Victoria in 1851. (The Festival Hall on the south bank of the Thames remains its chief monument.) Two years later (with Churchill back as Prime Minister) the coronation of a youthful Queen and the ascent of Everest, following on the apparent success of the Comet jet as well as the Viscount turbojet aircraft, were thought to symbolize the end of the time of troubles. The postwar revolution presaged, it was hoped, the emergence of a new and brighter Britain.

By British standards what had been accomplished in the fighting forties was in truth a revolution, a belated British version of the American New Deal and Russian five-year plans. The nation had girded itself for total war and had emerged victorious. It had then, apparently, transformed its social and economic structure. Businessmen welcomed the decision to reorganize the economy even if they distrusted the motives of the Labour party in insisting that this should be done through nationalized industries. Trade unionists and intellectuals hoped that the new society would help to overcome the class divisions which still cast a peculiar shadow over the claims of Britain to be a democracy. There was a widespread belief that as a result of the Welfare State the standard of living would be raised.

Yet by the early 1960s there was disappointment with what had been achieved: the revolution had been incomplete. The country had not entered a new zestful Elizabethan Age; instead the 1950s bore a strange resemblance to the 1930s in the alienation of the trade unions and the younger intellectuals from society. Worse still, the economy grew at only a painful 2½ percent per annum.[1] The diagnoses of the country's ills varied. On the Right some thought the postwar reforms a monstrous irrelevance; better to have had no revolution at all. On the Left there were those who thought that the Labour party did not go far enough, nationalizing a mere 20 percent of the economy and conveniently forgetting its promise to nationalize everything.

Both criticisms tended to ignore the fact that political parties respond to popular mood and circumstances. To accuse either party of responsibility for what went wrong is to be superficial. The causes of the malaise were much deeper, being partly the economic predicament in which the British found themselves as they tried to keep up appearances as one of the Great Powers, but even more the disinclination (or perhaps inability) of the people to create the sort of well-run economy whose products would be eagerly bought elsewhere. As always the British imported more than they exported, and increasingly imported manufactured goods of a type they could (and should) have made themselves.

The British achieved two main objects of the postwar Labour Government; full employment and greater social equality. But full employment was not an adequate substitute for a rapidly in-

---

[1] The growth rate 1958–1964 improved to 4 percent.

creasing gross national product. And despite increased equality Britain remained a highly class-conscious society.

Defeat in Victory: The Half-Revolution

Britain in 1945 was neither an affluent victor nor a ravaged battlefield. World War II galvanized the American economy, so much so that the gross national product in 1945 was double what it had been before the war. But for the defeated nations, and for the Russians, the war meant poverty, near-starvation and the wholesale destruction of the economy. Thanks to hard work and American economic aid most Western European countries put their economies together again by the early 1950s, building new plants, revaluing their currencies and occasionally writing off their debts.

The British stood alone in 1945 as they had in 1940. Like the Americans they were victors and thought themselves superior to the other nations of Europe which were defeated or occupied. It was not at first apparent that they too had been impoverished, since the Empire was still intact and London was still banker to the sterling area and the center of the Commonwealth. They soon found that in a competitive world they could not expect preferential treatment because of their wartime valor; they too had to work hard, to invest in new equipment and take a hard look at the future of sterling. Whereas other countries repudiated their debts, some for the second time in thirty years, Britain had now to add the colossal debt from World War II to World War I. By 1947 the national debt totaled £25 billion.

The British had obtained the foreign exchange needed for their war effort, until the advent of Lend Lease, by the sale of their dollar investments, often at a substantial discount on their true value. They had credited a number of countries, particularly Egypt and India, who had provided services for British forces during the war, with what came to be called sterling balances. Instead of scaling them down as part of the share of these countries to the Allied war effort, the British felt a moral duty to honor them. The

British were to feel cheated of the fruits of victory and were slow to recognize the success of their defeated trade rivals, Germany, Italy, and Japan (with whom the Americans seemed eager to be on good terms) in rebuilding their economies. Britain herself had few natural resources other than coal and the traditional skill of her people. The rich creditor nation of 1913 was now a debtor, to be forced in 1949 to devalue her currency for the second time (the first time being 1931 when she went off the gold standard), the pound becoming worth a mere $2.80. In such straitened circumstances it is hardly surprising that many of the plans laid in the early postwar era proved difficult to put into operation. The arms burden borne by Britain, and the amount of her aid to underdeveloped countries, particularly in the Commonwealth, was very heavy, totalling well over $6 billion a year. Nevertheless by 1965 the greater part of Britain's overseas investments had been retrieved and Britain was once again one of the world's largest creditor countries. The payments crisis caused the Government to curb this investment abroad.

It is difficult to assess the relative advantages enjoyed by the various European powers after 1945. The Germans and Italians did not have Britain's debts or arms burden, but on the other hand their economies were in poor shape at the end of the war. British industry was largely intact in 1945, there had been massive expansion in engineering and the other great export industries of the future, there was a highly trained workforce—and little competition from her prostrate rivals. Britain had a head start.

Unfortunately Britain was unable to exploit her advantage. The balance of trade, which had begun to work against her in the 1880s and had become such a problem in the 1930s, once again proved intractable. Her main raw material, coal, was in such short supply that it was the last commodity to be derationed— in 1958; then postwar mechanization produced enough coal. Her other basic domestic asset, steel, also remained in short supply throughout the period, at a time when Britain's steel could undersell that of her competitors. At times, both steel and coal were imported and the balance of payments was affected. By 1963 Japan was producing much more steel than Britain. In exports generally Britain gradually lost ground as a trading nation. In 1952–1953 Britain's share of world trade in manufactured goods was 22.2 percent compared with 22.4 percent in 1937. It was thought to have "levelled off" at about 14.8 percent in 1963 but it dropped to under 14 percent in 1964. Although she continued to be a leading importer, other countries seemed less dependent on her products than she was on theirs, a humiliating reversal of the nineteenth-century position. In 1964 the deficit was £756 million following one of £57 million in 1963. Unable to pay for her imports by exports, Britain was living beyond her means.[2]

The revolution therefore suffered partly because of Britain's delicate postwar economic condition and partly because the pace of change was not sustained. It also suffered because it was not always directed towards the right goals. In an era when the main emphasis should have been on increased production and productivity, a strong pound, a favorable balance of payments, attractive and stylish exports, and a stress on investment rather than consumption, successive Governments were mesmerised, apparently, by the twin spectres of the 1930s: unemployment at home and (to judge by the Suez crisis) appeasement abroad. Keynes's *General Theory of Employment, Interest and Money* (1936), which was designed to eliminate the unemployment of the 1930s, turned out to be the theoretical model for Britain in the postwar world. Instead of a dynamic approach to economics, typified by the new interest in economic growth, there was the essentially static analysis of the earlier British school. The main aim tended to be a more equitable distribution of wealth rather than an increase in production. This expressed itself in an emphasis on full employment even if this meant inflation, lower productivity and aid to declining areas. Business firms were induced to build plants in the so-called Development Areas and doctors were expected to move into the less attractive industrial areas. Instead of the profit motive there was the notion of the public interest, particularly under a Labour Government: the nationalized industries were ordered simply to make ends meet taking one year with

[2] In the first 9 months of 1965 the payments deficit was £353 million compared to £561 million in 1964—still very large.

another. In recent years this concept of the public interest has widened to mean a global public interest. A recent Labour apologist has pleaded for greater exports—in order that Britain can help underdeveloped countries to raise their standard of living. Instead of worrying about becoming poor relations among the countries of Western Europe and North America, many idealistic people in Britain are primarily concerned about the disparity between Britain's standard of living and that of the underdeveloped areas of the world. At the height of Britain's financial crisis in 1964 a Ministry of Overseas Development came into being.

By making full employment an end in itself instead of recognizing that it was the consequence of an economic policy primarily directed at growth and the promotion of exports, Britain cushioned itself at least temporarily against the grimly competitive atmosphere in which the rest of the world lived. Industries which failed to enter foreign markets were able to concentrate on the home market and make good profits. Wages were allowed, despite Government protests, to rise faster than productivity (by over 8 percent in 1964 alone). The Conservative Governments of 1951 to 1964 believed in the market as regulator rather than in direct controls over imports, but were hamstrung by the need to keep full employment if they were to retain popular support. The only alternative to deflation proved to be inflation, an evil apparently considered by the Conservative party to be preferable to a socialist victory. The old middle classes continued to vote Conservative out of dislike of socialism; the prosperous new middle class and many workers voted Conservative because they were doing well. But inflation was dangerous, particularly for an international currency like sterling, and loss of confidence could lead at any time to withdrawals of funds in London and the threat of sudden and possibly severe devaluation. For the fixed exchange rate meant that this traditional automatic corrective device no longer operated. Seventeen years after 1914 Britain devalued by leaving the gold standard; eighteen years after leaving the gold standard Britain devalued again; by 1965 another sixteen years had elapsed and a further adjustment could prove necessarily unless the economy changed direction. At the end of

the year exports were rising faster than imports, but the wage
spiral had not yet been halted.

Yet throughout the period, particularly the latter part, there
was the apparent paradox of a country prosperous internally and
yet externally beset by balance of payments crises. The British
standard of living was rising more slowly than that of many other
countries even though there was no absolute fall. Real prosperity
was largely the perquisite of those connected with the capital-
intensive manufacturing industries. What suffered most of all
was public investment. It was the public sector which the Government controlled and could restrict when a crisis came, and a
cut in public investment was less likely to arouse opposition than
a "pay pause." By the early 1960s the price paid for the policy
of postponing public investment became apparent and in early
1965 the Labour party announced cuts in private spending instead. But public spending was reduced in July.

Britain had taken a position in 1945 which made her recovery
rather different from the market economy of the United States
(and later of Western Germany, Italy, and Japan) and yet very
different from the command economies of the Communist world
(or later planned economy of France.) Indeed one reason why
hers was a half-revolution was that the Government tended to
take responsibility away from the business community, e.g., by
demanding full employment and giving way to the trade unions
over wage increases without providing adequate alternative
leadership. The Government even left the nationalized industries
in the hands of autonomous corporations, thus obscuring responsibility for unpopular decisions. For the most part, especially
after Cripps retired, it did not have a firm wages or price or
export policy. The pay pause of 1961 was a success mainly in those
parts of the public sector where the Government could bring
pressure to bear; least powerful were the university teachers, whose
salaries were determined by the Chancellor of the Exchequer
himself, anxious to set an example: his action intensified the
"brain drain" to North America.

In 1962 the National Economic Development Council was
set up and its companion, the National Incomes Commission,

reorganized in 1965 as the National Board for Prices and Incomes. But these were primarily attempts to examine the problem and help all parties to agree on the need to formulate a policy rather than instruments to enforce the Government's will. Despite the increasing importance of the civil service in directing the nation's affairs it remained an elite administration recruited mainly from among Oxford and Cambridge graduates. At the top the contrast between the professional businessmen in the United States performing the duties of Secretary of the Treasury and Secretary of Defense and the swift succession of professional politicians in British ministerial posts symbolized the different approach to the complex problems of modern adminstration.

Of course the Government was not solely to blame; the electors, trade unions and, above all, management must all take their share. (And the Labour Government, to its credit, did send productivity teams of both sides of industry to study American methods in the late 1940s and supported Cripps' stern measures of austerity.) But the Government must take most of the blame since it took the credit if things went well. Indeed the trouble was that the Government claimed the *responsibility* for policy, but failed to act decisively. Yet such was the nature of the half-revolution that it is doubtful whether either the politicians or the civil servants "responsible" would have been prepared to accept any blame at all.

The Price of a Half-Revolution

Enthusiasm in a revolutionary period of austerity is keyed up by the promise of Utopia tomorrow: once the cost of reform has been worked out a period of individual belt-tightening is ordered while the foundations are laid for future prosperity. Britain's half-revolution meant that after a brief period of "austerity" there was a general disinclination to believe that Britain had to copy the Russians or Germans rather than the affluent Americans and to sacrifice the consumer goods of the postwar world, particularly automobiles, television, and household appliances, in favor of long-term capital investment in such sectors as transport, fuel and power, housing, hospitals, and higher education. As we have seen, Cripps had already shown in 1949 that in times of crisis the government would find it simplest to limit investment and government expenditure. We shall have something to say about investment in all four sectors: transport, fuel and power, housing and hospital construction, and higher education.

TRANSPORT

The main forms of transport are roads, railways, ships, and aircraft. In the field of transport the preference for consumption over investment particularly manifested itself in road transport policy. Despite high taxes on vehicles and gasoline, no expressways were constructed in the American or European fashion before World War II. In 1946 a ten-year programme of 1000 miles of motorways was announced to cost, at the start, about £80 million a year. Two years later the necessary enabling legislation was passed, the Minister of Transport telling the Commons that no action would be taken until there were more favorable economic conditions. But he did remark that there were 3½ million vehicles on the roads and admitted that "we are hopelessly in arrears. Sooner or later we must tackle the problem unless we are to be choked to death by the motor vehicles on our roads." In 1948 road maintenance was still only 60 percent of the prewar average. In 1955 the Minister announced the start of motorway construction. In 1946 the plan called for 100 miles of motorway a year; when started in 1955 the rate was to be 43. In 1965 some 350 miles of motorway were in use. But by then nearly 11 million vehicles were on the roads, and parts of many trunk highways were still narrow, twisting two-lane roads. Just as the British were beginning to feel really "choked to death" the Buchanan Report on urban roads (1963) announced that the automobile age was only just beginning and that the number of vehicles would rise to 18 million in 1970 and 27 million in 1980. By increasing expenditure it was hoped that the 1946 target of 1000 miles of motorways would be reached in the early 1970s. The Thames Road Tunnel authorized in 1930, and the Forth Road Bridge authorized in 1947, have been completed but no motorway goes through any city, the 73-mile London-Birmingham motorway (M I) stopping well outside both cities. The 1959 Committee on London Roads remarked of urban expressways that "such ideas may well have a place in London in the future. It has not been possible for us to reach any conclusion in this report on the merits of any of these projects and in any event their construction is not feasible within the foreseeable financial limits." Yet it admitted that the last major piece of central-London road construction, of Kingsway and Aldwych, had taken place in 1905, and that since 1939 "money had been spent on other things." Motorways were possible according to Buchanan

Only if there is a disregard for all considerations other than the free flow of traffic which seems sometimes to be almost ruthless. Our British cities are not only packed with buildings, they are also packed with history, and to drive motorways through them on the American scale would inevitably destroy much that ought to be preserved.

By 1965 the first urban motorway, to London airport, was in operation.

For a time the British, who pioneered the railways, hoped to divert some of the traffic back to the railroads. In the same year that the motorway programme was announced (1955) a programme of railway modernization, including electrification of the midland route parallel to the chief motorway, was started and £1000 million was spent in eight years. Some time later it was discovered that equally important was the closure of a vast network (half the total) of uneconomic lines. But it proved difficult to overcome popular resistance to railway closure and the process was stopped by the new Labour Government in 1964. Many people seriously believed that Britain could not afford to ruin good agricultural land by the building of new roads. The contrast between the ruthless way the Victorians cut their railroads through the country and the timidity of the new Elizabethans in creating an adequate road network was startling.

If nothing could prevent the decline of the railways the same was not true of ships and shipbuilding. But here again it was foreign shipyards which obtained the orders, and foreign shipping

lines which built the largest new vessels to cross the Atlantic
(though lines like the P. & O. built a new fleet for the Far Eastern
service). In 1963 only 11 percent of new world shipping tonnage
was launched in British yards. About 220,000 persons were employed in this troubled industry. A report by the Department
of Scientific and Industrial Research indicated that conservative
techniques were partly to blame; 1965 saw an improvement.

Although Britain was apparently unable to adapt itself quickly
to new forms of transport on land and sea it nevertheless attempted
to be America's main competitor in aircraft construction. There
was initial success with the Viscount turboprop. Then in 1952
the Comet I was the first commercial jet aircraft, but three
crashes due to metal fatigue put an end to its challenge. In 1958
the Boeing 707 came into service at the same time as the Comet
IV and was superior in speed, number of passengers, and range.
But the British did not give up and staked a great deal on other
aircraft, in particular the VC-10. By 1964, when the final decision
to buy or cancel the VC-10 had to be made, BOAC asked if it
could cancel the 30 super VC-10s on order, retain the 12 VC-10s
already being delivered, and merely add six new Boeings to the
20 already in service. The Government decided against this proposal and compelled BOAC to buy seven super VC-10s in the
period 1964–1967 and another ten after 1967. (After this decision,
there were some doubts about the Concord, the proposed Anglo-
French superjet.) Unfortunately the British market alone was
unable to sustain a large aircraft industry, and having failed to
meet the competition of Douglas and Boeing the British Government decided in 1965 to reduce the size of the industry—
which employed 262,000 people. However, export sales rose by 55
percent (to $400 million) in 1965.

Britain's dilemma over the revolution in communications is not
peculiar to her. Everywhere railroads and shipping are threatened
by competition from motor vehicles and aircraft. What distinguishes Britain is an affection for railroads sufficient to delay
closure and reorganization, a reluctance to build enough modern
highways and expressways for the rapidly increasing number of
motor vehicles, a slow reaction to the modern shipbuilding
methods pioneered abroad, and the unsuccessful attempt to com-

pete with the Americans in the production of aircraft. The railways had a deficit of £150 million in 1962, road congestion was estimated to cost £500 million a year, while the sharp decline in export earnings of the shipbuilding and aircraft industries contributed to Britain's adverse balance of payments.

Aircraft and ships are built by private firms; roads and railways are ultimately the responsibility of the Ministry of Transport; all have encountered difficulties. There is no clear evidence that it is the public or the private sector which is the less enterprising. The Labour party is more deeply committed to the nationalized railways and the railwaymen than to the privately owned aircraft, shipbuilding, and road construction industries, and Mr. Harold Wilson criticized the Beeching Report on the need to reorganize the railways for its "narrow bookkeeping considerations."

FUEL AND POWER

Four main fuels are used in Britain: coal, gas, electricity, and oil (including gasoline). Since gas and electricity were largely derived from coal, the postwar rise in price and short supply of this basic fuel caused difficulties for both industries. It encouraged the switch to oil, which had to be imported from the Middle East (hence the importance of the Suez Canal). In 1964 the Gas Council begain importing natural gas and the Electricity Authority started constructing power stations based on nuclear power. Then the demand for coal fell and this form of fuel became plentiful again. The problem facing the Government, which controlled the coal, gas, and electricity industries but not oil, was whether to encourage the use of domestic coal in order to aid the balance of payments or whether to allow industry to buy what was cheapest in the international market, i.e., oil.

By 1963 crude oil formed the largest single imported item and cost £382 million. In the same year the National Coal Board's accumulated deficit was £90 million. Oil imports had risen by a third in three years. From a strategic as well as a financial point of view this dependence on foreign sources of energy was considered unwise but it was realized that coal was no longer the best form of fuel.

The British Government had already decided that the best

alternative to both coal and oil was electricity generated either by coal or by nuclear power and one of the world's largest nuclear power programmes was put under way. By 1963 11 percent of all Britain's gross fixed capital formation—£554 million—was in electricity supply, over six times as much as was spent on either coal or gas, and 10,000 MW of nuclear power was planned. (Total generating capacity was 36,523 MW in 1963.) There are indications that this decision will prove a sound one.

Before 1914 Britain was one of the world's great exporters of fuel in the form of 90 million tons of coal annually. Since 1945 she has been increasingly dependent on imports of oil. In the 1970s she will, it is hoped, have an ample supply of cheap electric power. (This helps to explain why money was invested in railway electrification rather than expressways.) At the time of writing the big question is whether oil and natural gas will be discovered in large quantities in the North Sea near the shores of Britain.

It is now clear that after 1945 an efficient coal industry, on which both gas and electricity utilities were originally based, would have greatly reduced the drain on Britain's foreign exchange reserves. From now onwards, much depends on the country's heavy investment in nuclear power as a domestically produced alternative to coal. Because of its commitments to the nationalized coal industry and the miners, the Labour party has been less willing than the Conservatives to permit coal-mining to contract, though another deficit in 1965 led to drastic reorganization of the Coal Board. But both parties are committed to the development of nuclear power.

HOUSING AND HOSPITAL CONSTRUCTION

Nowhere has the half-revolution in Britain revealed itself so clearly as in the building of dwellings and hospitals (and other public buildings). Although the post-1918 "Homes for Heroes" never materialized, the construction industry prospered in the 1930s. The prewar rate of housebuilding was not to be matched until the very end of the period 1945–1965. For much of the period there seemed to be a shortage of bricks (like coal and steel a domestic product). At first housing was also limited by building restrictions. In the 1950s the cost of mortgages rose by 50 percent or more because of high interest rates (which particularly affected those houses which were bought by means of fixed interest mortgages). More recently land speculation and rising costs in a relatively inefficient industry which lacked foreign competition created a difficult problem. The rate of slum-clearance, though at a record 76,000 dwellings in 1962, will have to be doubled and after 1975 trebled if the country is to keep pace with the legacy of nineteenth-century speculative building. Yet after 1953–1954 the rate of housebuilding declined for the next ten years. While over 5 million dwellings were built in the period 1945–1965, the average was only 270,000 a year. The rebuilding proceeded at a far slower rate than that of Germany. The Labour party has promoted public housing, the Conservatives private construction.

As for hospitals, although there was considerable modernization of existing facilities, no new ones were built between 1939 and 1960, typifying the widespread notion that existing capital equipment could be used indefinitely and that the main need was not production of new equipment but the redistribution of existing resources. Only towards the end of the period did the implications of this failure to consider technological obsolescence become clear. The 1960 ten-year £500 million programme of hospital construction was a crash programme not fully thought out: within two years the cost had to be revised from £500 million to £750 million. Even so, a hundred major schemes had to be postponed, most of them beyond 1975. In the ten years 1948–1958 only £100 million had been spent on hospital improvements.

EDUCATION

The British are proud of their accomplishments in school construction since 1945; 8000 schools were built in the years 1947–1964 and many reforms carried out. The reports of the Ministry of Education reflect this sense of achievement. Yet the success of this Ministry is outstanding only if it is compared with other British services; compared to the problems of rapid expansion of school populations in many other countries Britain's problems

Table 4.1. Number of Houses and Apartments Built in Britain

Date	Party in Power	Built by Public Authorities	Built by Private Enterprise	Total
1951	Labour	166,483	25,485	201,856
1954	Conservative	239,318	92,423	354,129
1958	Conservative	145,547	128,148	273,695
1962	Conservative	130,628	174,800	305,428
1963	Conservative	124,008	174,864	298,872
1964	Conservative	155,582	218,094	373,676
1965	Labour	168,498	213,799	382,297
1945–1965		3,207,255	2,139,232	5,346,487

NOTE: In Scotland only 77,009 dwellings out of a total of 564,130 built in 1945–1965 were built by private owners.
SOURCE: *Housing Return for Scotland, 31st December, 1965*, Edinburgh: Her Majesty's Stationery Office (Command Paper 2885), 1966.

are hardly terrifying. The Province of Ontario, Canada, was building schools at almost the same rate, with a total population one-eighth the size. And despite the building programme a third of all schoolchildren in Britain were in oversize classes in 1962. The discrimination between children of academic and nonacademic ability at the early age of eleven persisted, and the school-leaving age, raised to 15 in 1947, had still not been raised to 16. The first step, that of giving all children the opportunity of going to a senior school from 11 to 15 was not quite completed in 1964. The second step, of giving a high school education to all, awaits the 1970s. Despite the creation of new universities, the places available have not proved sufficient to meet the need, and so university education probably will not come into its own until the 1970s or even 1980s. The aim has been to double university enrolment between 1951 and 1971. (In Canada the enrolment doubled between 1958 and 1964 and will double again between 1964 and 1971.)

By 1965 the strength of a country's economy was coming to be measured by its gold reserves as well as its exports, old-fashioned though this may seem to be. Over 90 percent of Britain's reserves were in gold and the following table speaks for itself. Table 1.2 in Chapter One indicated that in consumption standards, though not in growth, Britain was still ahead of the countries of the European Economic Community by 1960. The following table indicates that in gold reserves Britain was falling behind. Also by 1965 most of Britain's official currency "reserves" consisted largely of money borrowed from the International Monetary Fund—nearly $3 billion.

Table 4.2. Gold Reserves in Millions of Dollars

	1955	1963	1965
United Kingdom	2012	2484	2111
Six countries of the European Economic Community	4007	12333	14514

In this chapter we have compared the promise of 1945 with the performance attained by 1965. The Labour party which believed in planning in 1945 was abandoning it in 1951; the Conservatives who did not believe in it ended the period by regarding it as an unwelcome necessity. Despite everything, British consumers emerged apparently far richer than they had been two decades earlier. But it was still doubtful whether the nation's prosperity was solidly based; the 1964–1965 financial crisis was the worst since devaluation in 1949. Neither political party had come to grips with the deep-seated malaise of the British economy. And although the parliamentary system of government should not take all the blame it was at least arguable that it had failed to carry through the economic and social revolution envisaged in 1945.

Writing in the 1950s about the second Labour Government of 1929–1931, Mr. Herbert Morrison, a former Labour Cabinet minister, observed that though life was made particularly difficult by the "world economic blizzard," it was made harder, he said "by the relatively primitive character of government organization at that time, having regard to the problems the Government was expected to face."

Yet the parliamentary system had been in existence for centuries by 1929. Today there are still complaints that the machinery of government is inadequate for the problems which ministers must face. Ultimately the British political system will be judged abroad by its capacity to overcome its difficulties.

It is difficult to know if anyone is to blame for Britain's economic predicament. Some observers indict the Labour party for its failure to realize that its preoccupation with social legislation has led to loss of confidence in the financial world at home and abroad. Others, with perhaps more justification in view of the Labour Government's proved record of austerity from 1945 to 1951, accuse the Conservatives of pandering to the people over wage settlements when Britain needed to place greater emphasis (1951–1964) on capital investment, economic growth, and greater productivity. (The slogan "You never had it so good" is said to have helped the Conservatives win the 1959 election.) Foreigners tend to blame the nation as a whole for thinking it could have its cake and eat it. History alone will show whether any political party could have arrested Britain's decline. A people which loses confidence in its future has at least some justification for trying to get the most satisfaction out of the present.

The events of 1964–1965 did not culminate in the reversion of the two main parties to their traditional roles—the Right for fiscal orthodoxy and deflation and the Left for deficit financing and inflation. Certainly the Labour party is afraid of once again being identified with austerity: the Conservatives are afraid of being identified with the unemployment of the 1930s. But at the end of 1965 neither party had much choice. Both austerity and unemployment were distinct possibilities if Britain was to pay off her debts and re-establish confidence in sterling. Once again the debt payments to Canada and the United States were postponed and $1000 million had to be repaid to the International Monetary Fund by the end of 1967, with another $1500 million to be paid back in the following three years.

By March, 1966 it seemed doubtful whether these sums could be repaid on time. Britain's gold and currency reserves in September, 1964 had totalled $3029 million. In addition, there was a dollar portfolio worth $1414 million which gave the government total reserves of $4443 million. A year later, as a result of borrowing $2382 million from the IMF and Swiss banks, the net reserves amounted to $1787 million. In March, 1966, a month before the election, the Chancellor of the Exchequer announced that Britain had nearly $5 billion in reserve. But of these, $2520 million were in loans, $1000 million unused credit in New York, and only $1632 million gold and currency reserves. In fact, Britain's net reserves had declined in eighteen months from $4443 million to $888 million. This takes no account of the $6000 million of sterling balances, i.e., liabilities to countries in the sterling area, or the post-war American and Canadian loans, for which payments of a further $6000 million were outstanding.

CHAPTER FIVE

The Administration of the Nation's Affairs

> Britain has left the epoch of classical parliamentary government, and entered a new epoch of bureaucratic democracy—with its new division between the dignified and efficient elements in the constitution.
>
> R. H. S. Crossman

AT ONE TIME people seemed to go about their business without too much reference to the government and its servants. Of course there always was a need for men to serve in the armed forces; at every port there were customs and excise men; and there were numerous industrious clerks such as the great Samuel Pepys ensuring that the national finances were being properly looked after.

Today all this is changed. The number of persons directly or indirectly employed by government runs into millions and it is important to devote a chapter to administration not only because this is more important than ever, but because the ramifications of the civil service, local government, and the machinery of justice enter into everyone's daily lives.

The Civil Service

WHAT IT COMPRISES

British government is divided into two areas—central and local government. These may be contrasted with the three American levels—federal, state, and local. The civil service is the term used to describe national civil administration and it excludes the armed forces, the police, the employees of nationalized industries, and local government officials. Civil servants have been defined as "those servants of the Crown, other than holders of political or judicial offices, who are employed in a civil capacity, and whose remuneration is paid wholly and directly out of monies voted by Parliament." [1] This strict definition does, however, include one large class of civil servants who are often overlooked—the *industrial* civil servants who work in arsenals, dockyards, or the Post Office.

The numbers involved in the public service are indicated in Table 5.1.

ITS CLASS STRUCTURE

Like bureaucracies everywhere the British civil service forms a pyramid, the base of which supports a comparatively small number of senior civil servants (in what is called the higher civil service composed mainly of the administrative class) who help ministers to determine policy. It is these men (and women) who are primarily responsible for the administration of the nation's affairs. What determines the particular shape of the British pyramid? How does it differ from the American?

The most distinctive feature of the British civil service is its class structure; and in particular the concentration of power in a small administrative class of under 3000 people. Many of these "mandarins" are educated at Oxford and Cambridge and enter the administrative class by special examination after obtaining their bachelor of arts degree. By moving from one department to another they obtain a broad view of governmental problems and soon develop an attachment to the service of which they form the proud elite. Behaving almost as a distinct caste they have been largely incorruptible, loyal, hardworking, and able. Until recently they were regarded as a model to the rest of the world. Table 5.2 gives some indication of the structure of a government department.

[1] W. J. M. Mackenzie and J. W. Grove, *Central Administration in Britain*, London: Longmans, 1957, p. 11.

Table 5.1. The Public Service: Employed Population

I. The Civil Service

A. The nonindustrial Civil Service

Class	Staff Group	Jan. 1, 1965
1. Administrative	Administrative (Home) including Diplomatic Service	3,462
2. Executive	General Executive and Departmental Executive	77,747
3. Clerical	General Clerical and Departmental Clerical	130,128
4. Ancillary Clerical	Clerical Assistants and Typing Grades	97,675
5. Messengerial	Messengerial, etc.	34,201
6. Specialist	Professional, Scientific and Technical I, Scientific and Technical II, Ancillary Technical	131,601
7. Inspectorate	Inspectorate	2,837
8. Post Office	Post Office Minor and Manipulative	218,430
	Total whole-time nonindustrial Civil Service	696,081

B. The Industrial Civil Service | 246,000

	April 1965
Armed Forces	
Army	194,000
Navy	100,000
Air Force	132,000
Total	426,000

3. Nationalized Industries	
Total number June, 1961	2,196,000
4. Local Government Service	755,000

SOURCE: U.K. Central Statistical Office and H.M. Treasury, London, S.W. 1.

Today the British civil service is frequently criticized. It is said to cherish its amateur status in a world which is becoming increasingly professionalized. Although the undergraduate education which they receive is still excellent by international standards, British administrators have often lacked the postgraduate or professional training which in many other countries follows the award of a B.A. The absence of scientists, lawyers, engineers—and even of specialists in economics, sociology, or political science—is said to put the civil service at a disadvantage in dealing with business firms or foreign powers. A man who has not received any specialized training is unlikely to keep abreast of a rapidly changing scientific and technological world (unless he is admirably advised by those who have such competence).

Table 5.2. Departmental Structure:
Senior Officials of the Treasury, August, 1965

Administrative Class
   2 Joint Permanent Secretaries (one is head of the Civil Service)
   3 Second Secretaries
   1 Head of the Government Economic Service
   1 Economic Adviser to the Treasury
   6 Third Secretaries
  15 Under-Secretaries
  41 Assistant Secretaries
  71 Principals
  12 Assistant Principals

Executive Class
   1 Principal Executive Officer
   4 Senior Chief Executive Officers
  29 Chief Executive Officers
   8 Senior Organization Officers
  53 Senior Executive Officers
  31 Organization Officers

SOURCE: U.K. Central Statistical Office and H.M. Treasury, London, S.W. 1.

A second criticism is that the service is attuned to an earlier era when government was mainly regulatory; it is not, so the critics allege, geared to a highly competitive world where civil servants have to be as smart as businessmen and as willing to take risks and initiate new programmes. The problems faced by the civil service have changed—for example it is more important to balance one's international payments than one's internal budget —but the civil service has not always changed its methods or personnel to meet them. It may well be that an academically trained civil servant cloistered in Whitehall since graduation is not necessarily the best person to supervise defense contracts in the rough and tumble of the world of business.

In addition to the criticism of the amateur status of the civil servant and his concern for administrative tidiness rather than entrepreneurial innovation there is a third which challenges the whole hierarchical class structure on which the civil service is based. It is suggested that the hierarchy of the administrative class (of university graduates), executive class (high school graduates) and clerical class (educated to the age of 15) is out of date and too reminiscent of Plato's Republic with its rulers, auxiliaries, and artisans. British society is no longer divided into fairly rigid classes: it is more egalitarian, more mobile, and more professionally oriented. As evidence may be cited the growth of the specialist class outside the traditional Treasury hierarchy and to a large extent denied access to positions of responsibility: the expert, so it is argued, "should be on tap, not on top." Yet the specialists are the second largest of the classes and twice as large as the administrative and executive classes combined.

One of many incidents reveals the weakness of the existing structure. In 1964 when Ferranti Ltd. were accused of making excessive profits on the Bloodhound missile, it was found that the two largest contracts were checked by a Technical Grade I officer earning about $4000 a year. None of the technical cost officers had had personal practical experience in the manufacturing of electronic equipment. The Contracts Directorate staff normally accepted the estimates recommended by their technical cost colleagues who were presumed to be experts in this field. The senior administrators in the Ministry of Aviation were from the administrative class, not the specialist classes, and so were unable to ascertain what was going on.

Criticism should not obscure the fact that the British Empire has been served by a devoted group of men since the reforms of a hundred years ago, men whose esprit de corps has enabled them to resist the pressures which have damaged the civil service in so many less fortunate countries. Appointments are made not through patronage but after examination by a six-man Civil Service Commission. In return for such loyal service—to the civil service as a whole, not to a particular department—the civil servant has had security of tenure and has been awarded a pension and often a place in the Honours List. The senior civil servant, particularly, has a high social status, and the leading men in the Treasury (the Department which controls the others) are called "Treasury knights."

There are indications that the British civil service is adapting itself to changing conditions and the body which was for decades an object of universal admiration may be in the process of rejuvenation. Commissions of inquiry have been set up at frequent intervals and the result has been numerous reforms. For example British public accounts are now presented in a fashion much more comprehensible to the layman and as a result of the Plowden report *Control of Public Expenditure* (Cmnd. 1432) [2] surveys of a sort are made annually of proposed government expenditure for several years ahead.

It is being increasingly questioned whether the country can afford the luxury of amateur politicians superimposed on amateur civil servants who may themselves be out of sympathy with the professional expertise which is increasingly essential in every walk of life. There used to be some pride in the fact that one-third of the administrative class had risen from the executive grade. This was no doubt a step towards equality of opportunity and was lauded on that account. But what the British did not see is that it was a retrograde step *professionally*. Instead of adding graduate qualifications to the bachelors' degrees held by present-day senior civil servants form Oxford and Cambridge, they were introducing people who had no university education at all. The

[2] Her Majesty's Stationery Office, *Command Paper (Cmnd.) 1432*, 1961.

growth of the specialized class suggests that a greater degree of professionalism is nowadays expected elsewhere in the service.

WHERE DOES THE CIVIL SERVICE OPERATE?

We have already indicated that the civil service is a national organization, even though it excludes both local government and the nationalized industries. It therefore follows that by and large it is based on London and it is there that the main decisions have to be taken. The civil service is not in the City of London (which is the eastern business district) but in the City of Westminster which is near the West End. Whitehall, the street where the main government departments are, is close to Westminster and St. James's Palace which was once the residence of the monarch. Senior civil servants, ministers and MPs can, if they choose, lunch in one another's company at the same clubs in Pall Mall. Not all the great offices of state are in Whitehall: Customs and Excise appropriately enough is in the City of London, while several modern departments are in buildings elsewhere.

By no means all civil servants work in the capital, even if policy decisions are still largely made there. In Scotland and Northern Ireland there are fully staffed departments dealing with such matters as agriculture and pensions, and some decentralization of policy-making is inevitable. During World War II there was the creation of a system of Regional Commissioners on whom certain administrative tasks were devolved, but these were not continued after the war. (Like Cromwell's major-generals, they were useful in an emergency but went against the grain so far as local self-government was concerned.) Recently there have been proposals to introduce something comparable to this administrative system: if they are adopted they will bring Britain more in line with continental practice where local government is not always local self-government. The French Prefects spring to mind.

Decentralization of power is not to be confused with decentralization of routine administration. This has already occurred on a large scale in order to prevent the accumulation of unnecessary clerical staffs in London. The introduction of computers may reduce the size of the staffs dealing with such matters as pensions and national insurance; the remnant may one day come back to the capital. There are good reasons for the decentralization of routine functions, but to disperse those responsible for making decisions to the other end of the kingdom serves no purpose at all.

ITS EFFECTIVENESS

Traditionally the civil service has been a smooth-operating machine—or so we are led to believe. It is hard to be sure because those who write with authority on the subject tend to be senior civil servants or academicians who have served in the civil service during the war and are part of the "network." Senior civil servants frequently become heads of Oxford and Cambridge colleges and the connection between the public service and the universities is a close one at the top level. A number of American and Commonwealth observers have been admitted to the charmed circle and made to feel at home, with the result that they are tempted to adopt the official view that the British civil service is excellent.

Occasionally, however, there are indications that the picture which is painted may be too rosy. There are occasional "affairs" (e.g., the 1954 Crichel Down scandal) out of which the civil service emerges with something less than a clean slate. Those critics who have argued that the service may not be so remarkable after all are beginning to gain a hearing. Nothing has drawn more public attention to the workings of the service than the security cases of recent years. It has become apparent that the screening and supervision is not as adequate as it was thought to be, while the British security service, long considered (like the diplomatic service) to be the best in the world, was clearly capable of doing a botched job. Mr. Profumo's lies to the House of Commons, despite the comic overtones of his affair, shocked the public. It seemed that confidence in ministers because they came from the same social class could be taken too far. The "old-boy network"—another myth which has been widely accepted in Britain's organic society—was not apparently a guarantee of superior mental or moral capacity.

Three specific deficiencies, in addition to its generalist and hierarchic structure, may be mentioned. The first is that the civil service never overcame the legacy of penny-pinching which characterized the Victorian notion of how to run an empire. The Victorians managed to pile up immense fortunes and at the same time provide a competent civil, diplomatic and Indian service, each of which was run on a shoestring. To this day the civil service uses cheap yellow paper and Manila envelopes, some of which are used again with economy labels. Were the civil service to be performing only its traditional tasks this would not perhaps matter too much, but in the world of the Welfare State it sets the tone for a considerable area of public activity. How can the National Health Service or the universities expect to provide more than minimum standards if the Treasury's standards are so low? By "emancipating" a large sector (now the public sector) of the economy from business influence the Labour Government of 1945–1951 may inadvertently have inaugurated a lowering of standards which was to result in an extraordinary discrepancy between the affluent expense-account businessman and the struggling public servant. Not surprisingly (especially now that Britain is no longer the greatest power in the world) it is becoming more difficult to recruit able men to the public service.

The second deficiency has been an inadequate appreciation of the security problem. The absurd aspects of the McCarthy era in the United States concealed from the British the fact that in both countries the cold war demanded constant attention to the problem of security. But whereas the American government responded to pressure, much to the dismay of many liberals, the British regarded the fuss as overdone. They tended to underestimate the significance of a succession of security cases (the scientists Fuchs, Nunn May, and Pontecorvo, the diplomats Burgess, Maclean, and Philby) and refused to become alarmed. Their concern for the liberty of the individual was admirable, but whether there was adequate concern for the security of the nation is more doubtful. Fear of upsetting the morale of the service led the Government to tread warily; but perhaps a short-term dip in morale might have been helpful in preserving it in the long run.

The third possible deficiency is the very neutrality of the service and its willingness to serve any party which is in power. Observers were impressed by its enthusiasm in promoting the nationalization policies of the 1945–1951 Labour Government even though (so it was assumed) many senior civil servants were not socialists. But what they overlooked was that the civil servants, like anyone else, welcomed extensions of their sphere of influence, and the Labour Government was simply expanding their power. Presumably any government, even an extremist one, would require the aid of the bureaucracy, and the impartiality and neutrality of the civil service could become a problem if Britain faced a crisis similar to those of Germany in 1932 or Rhodesia in 1965.

Local Government

ITS STRUCTURE

Local government in Britain is embarking on its second major reform. Until the early nineteenth century local government in England and Wales was carried on in rural parishes by the local gentry acting as justices of the peace, and in the towns by corporations or vestries usually oligarchic in character.

Between 1835 and 1888 the first reform of the system took place to keep pace with the industrialization of the country. Local government was reorganized and democratized, first in the towns (the Municipal Corporations Act of 1835) and then in the counties and in London (Local Government Act of 1888). Broadly speaking, the country was divided into counties and county boroughs. Today, as a result of this second phase of development there are three distinct patterns of local government in the United Kingdom; the 67 administrative counties [3] and 85 county boroughs of England, Wales, and Northern Ireland; Greater London with its Council; and the 33 counties and 198 burghs (towns) in Scotland. But all these "local authorities," as they are called, have one characteristic in common: each is di-

[3] A large geographical county like Yorkshire comprises three administrative counties—the North, West, and East Ridings.

rectly responsible to the central government in London, Edinburgh, or Belfast.

There is one important difference between the county boroughs and counties. The county borough councils, representing sizable cities of 100,000 or more, are all-purpose authorities dealing with all local services delegated by act of Parliament to local jurisdiction—education, police, roads, etc. But the county councils, as might be expected of bodies responsible for comparatively large areas, do not try to administer every service in the county. A number are delegated to smaller local authorities which vary in their powers according to their size and resources. Some are boroughs (towns) of over 50,000 which are administered by borough councils (not to be confused with county boroughs which as their name implies have the status of counties), some are urban districts, while the authorities with least power are the rural districts—though these are further subdivided into 10,800 parishes.

The two distinctive features of the geographical distribution of British local authorities, therefore, have been the division of the country into counties and county boroughs, and the further subdivision of the counties so that they enjoy a two-tier system of local government.

The second reform phase, which has just begun, is taking the form of a trend towards regional government. The Greater London Council is responsible for the whole of the metropolitan area, and regional governments are foreshadowed for other parts of the country which are heavily industrialized. Just as the growth of industrial towns in the nineteenth century led to the separation of the county boroughs from the counties, so the emergence of the conurbations, to use the British term, has meant the creation of a system of government specifically designed for the modern metropolitan area. The new trend was foreshadowed in the period 1945–1950 when many public services, e.g., hospitals and electric and gas utilities, were transferred from local authorities to the new nationalized industries which in turn set up administrative regions of their own. Larger units of local government are thought to have many advantages.

SERVICES PROVIDED

Local authority services are classified under three heads: environmental, protective, and personal. The *environmental* services include drains and sewers, street cleaning and garbage disposal, water supply, and measures to prevent air pollution and ensure food hygiene. Highway (except national highway) construction, street lighting, parks and recreation grounds all fall within local jurisdiction, and it is the local authority which is responsible for town and country planning.

Under the heading of *protective* services fall the police, fire service, and civil defense. *Personal* services include various health programmes not transferred to the National Health Service; for example, the ambulance service and the provision of entertainment (where this is undertaken). The most important personal services are housing and education. Over 60 percent of the dwellings built 1945–1965 were built by local authorities, although from 1954 to 1964 the Conservatives increased the proportion of privately built homes to over half the total. Greater emphasis on slum clearance and urban renewal has more recently led to a larger role by the local authority.

Although over half a million children attend private schools, 12 out of 13 boys and girls are enrolled in public schools operated by local authorities. Of the religious denominations in England only the Catholics still have a considerable number (about 2000) of "voluntary" schools, but even these are under the jurisdiction of local authorities which actually maintain them. (English Catholics must pay part of the cost of maintenance of buildings.) Teachers' salaries are determined by national organizations although teachers are appointed and dismissed by local authorities which delegate this responsibility to their Education Committees.

There are many other services provided by local authorities but one thing characterizes the overwhelming proportion of them: they are administered under act of Parliament and therefore are of fairly uniform standards throughout the country. Altogether local authorities employ over a million people, including about 330,000 teachers.

HOW LOCAL GOVERNMENT IS DIRECTED AND FINANCED

Local authorities in England and Wales are in the hands of councillors elected for three years and aldermen elected by the councillors for six. None has the strong single executive common in the United States. In county boroughs the Mayor or Lord Mayor is merely the presiding officer. (The counties, at both levels of government, have chairmen, not mayors.) The political organization is neither parliamentary nor presidential in character but follows the convention model. The council carries on its business through powerful committees, particularly the Finance Committee, and with the help of full-time officials who are career officers appointed by the council. These move from one authority to another as they climb up the local government administrative hierarchy to senior administrative positions.

The officials in local government are much more like American administrators than like the administrative class of the civil service. Instead of being products of an Oxford or Cambridge liberal education, they are professionally trained lawyers, engineers, educators, surveyors, accountants, etc. By and large it may be said that the caliber of local government officials is high, especially in the large authorities. By comparison the status of councillors is somewhat low and would be still lower were not the councils the breedings ground of members of Parliament, particularly in the Labour party. The nonpartisan councillor has now become much less conspicuous. Today most councils are divided into groups which in the main reflect the national parties. The defeat of many Labour candidates in the 1947 local elections was a sign that all was not well with the Labour Government of 1945–1950.

Local authorities obtain their income from central government grants and from money which they raise themselves via property taxation or loans. The largest single grant is the general grant paid by the Minister of Housing and Local Government to county and county borough councils and by the Secretary of State for Scotland to county and town councils in Scotland. In the 1963–1964 estimates it amounted to £794 million or 13 percent of the national budget. An interesting feature of the grant is that it is determined by a formula based on the size and density of the population and the number of children and old people. Local authorities raise over a third of their income themselves through property taxes, the "rates." Property is valued by the Board of Inland Revenue but the tax is determined by the local authority each year. Rates are criticized as a regressive form of taxation unsuited for an expanding economy. Things have been made worse in England by the total exemption of agricultural land and buildings and the partial exemption (until 1963) of industrial property. Consequently until recently private householders have paid about half the total rates, which in 1960–1961 yielded £697 million. But the system of supplementary government grants enables the central government to control local policy. Capital expenditure is financed by loans. Authorities may raise money in a variety of ways but both the loans and the actual schemes must be sanctioned by the central government. Authorities which cannot raise money themselves on reasonable terms may apply to the Public Works Loan Board.

THE CONTROL OF LOCAL GOVERNMENT

The central government has many powers of control over local authorities. Legally, these authorities can be challenged in the courts if they exceed their powers. Administratively they must conform to departmental directives which supplement acts of Parliament, and many of their appointments and dismissals, e.g., of Chief Constable and Medical Officer of Health, have to be approved by the central government. In financial matters they must conform to the directives issued from government departments when grants-in-aid are provided. Inspectors and District Auditors appointed by the Ministry of Housing and Local Government keep a close watch on local affairs. The British seem to approve of this arrangement because it ensures a high level of administration whatever the composition of the local council and because it avoids some of the irregularities found in certain American cities and counties. But the price of good administration is a high degree of central control and often a lack of that independent grass roots initiative which is such a marked feature of the best

American local units of government. That the system survives is due to a remarkable degree of personal cooperation between the officials of the two levels of government.

ADMINISTRATIVE EFFICIENCY VERSUS LOCAL PARTICIPATION: RECENT TRENDS

With effect from April 1st, 1965, the government of Greater London was reorganized and so great was the extension of the authority of the former London County Council (to be known in future as the Greater London Council) that the administrative county of Middlesex ceased to exist. Twelve inner and twenty outer London boroughs, and the City of London, continued to exercise certain powers, but overall authority was vested in what in effect was a regional government covering 620 square miles and with a population of eight million. It is possible that similar systems of regional administration will be introduced in other metropolitan areas. The argument in favor of amalgamation of the existing authorities is administrative efficiency, and there are many observers who regard the present system (see Table 5.3) as archaic. Opposition to the change does not seem to come primarily from voters' organizations anxious to preserve participation in politics at the local level. This may be because there is relatively little popular interest in local government.

The main decisions affecting citizens are made by the central government and as we have seen some important services have already been transferred to nationalized industries and their regional organizations. In the counties themselves, power has tended to pass to the upper of the two tiers of government. The "vested interests" opposed to change are not the city corporations, rotten-borough proprietors and ad hoc bodies of the nineteenth century but the various elected borough councils who would like to retain their faded prestige. It seems that in the long run they will lose.

Over the next five years interest will no doubt center on the new regions. Although it is too early to assess their significance, there are indications that an attempt will be made to coordinate the activities of the nationalized industries in their various regions with the new regional councils and incorporate both into

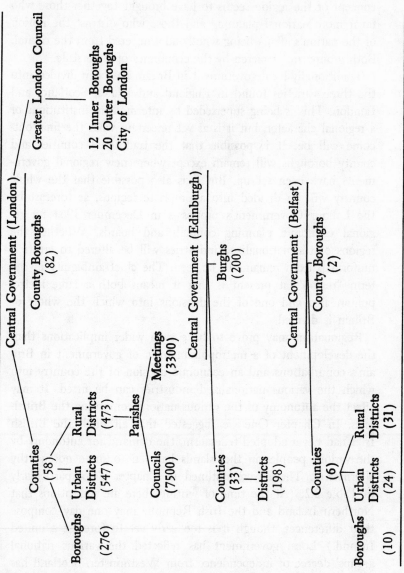

NOTE: There are proposals for a new system of regional-local government on the London pattern for several metropolitan areas.

the national framework for planned economic growth. Indeed the concept of the region seems to have brought together those who favor more national planning and those who distrust the notion of the nation's affairs being wholly administered from the capital. Both groups are attracted by the economies of large scale.

Traditionally local government in Britain has been divided into the three varieties found in England and Wales, Scotland, and London. This is being superseded by intermediate institutions of a regional character, but it is as yet uncertain what the final outcome will be. It is possible that the traditional counties and county boroughs will remain except where new regional governments have been set up. But it is also possible that the whole country will be divided into appropriate regions, as forecast by the Labour Government's proposals in December 1964 for regional economic planning councils and boards. Whether the regions of the nationalized industries will be altered to create a uniform pattern remains to be seen. The chief ambiguity in the term "region" at present is that it means both a large metropolitan area and one of the divisions into which the whole of Britain is divided.

Regionalism may prove to have even wider implications than the development of a metropolitan form of government in Britain's conurbations and an economic division of the country into which the various nationalized industries can be fitted. It may affect the autonomy of the various nations composing the British Isles. In Chapter One we suggested that although the British Isles had never adopted federalism, the demand for autonomy by the various peoples in the islands had led to some noteworthy alternatives. These were outlined in Chapter Two, particularly in Table 2.2. (At the time of writing there are indications that Northern Ireland and the Irish Republic may one day compose their differences, though it is too early yet to forecast a united Ireland.) Local government has reflected the various national groups' degree of independence from Westminster. Scotland has its own traditional system of local government based in Edinburgh. Northern Ireland has the English system but it is based in Belfast. Wales not only shares the English system but has it based in London like English local government. The Scots and the Ulster Irish complain that they do not receive adequate help from London to cure their economic ills, while the Welsh resent the fact that they have no national capital comparable to Belfast and Edinburgh.

The trend towards regional government could meet both objections. If the whole of the United Kingdom were divided into regions (England being subdivided), there might be less complaint that England is favored over Scotland and Northern Ireland. If Wales were to become a region of its own this might meet the nationalists' demand for greater Welsh self-government.

Law and Order

THE COURTS

Table 5.4 outlines the court structure in England, Wales, and Northern Ireland, which have been connected since the twelfth century. Scotland, which has been united to England for only 250 years, retains its own legal system which is quite different. There are no equivalents in England of the sheriffs and procurators-fiscal, and Scottish common law is based on Roman law, not on English common law. Even on paper the British legal system is not very tidy, while in practice it is far less easy to understand. All that the student who is merely being introduced to British government needs to do, however, is to ask himself the question: What are the main courts?

There are five main levels. At the top there is the House of Lords (and Judicial Committee of the Privy Council), the final court of appeal. Below the Lords are two appeal courts, the Court of Appeal and Court of Criminal Appeal. (The House of Lords accepts appeals only on points of law.) Below the Courts of Appeal are the High Court of Justice (mainly civil) and the Assize (criminal) courts. The fourth rung in the ladder is occupied by county courts for civil cases and Quarter Sessions for criminal offences. At the bottom are petty sessions, juvenile courts and the magistrates' courts of summary jurisdiction.

Table 5.4. Court Structure in England and Wales

House of Lords
Lord Chancellor, Legal Peers, and 9 Lords of Appeal in Ordinary
Appeals in civil and criminal cases involving a point of law of general public importance.

CIVIL COURTS	CRIMINAL COURTS
Court of Appeal The Master of Rolls and Lord Justices of Appeal (not less than 8 nor more than 11) Appeals in civil cases from County Courts or High Court of Justice. May send to another lower court for a fresh trial or reconsider evidence itself but without fresh testimony.	**Court of Criminal Appeal** 3 judges of Queen's Bench Appeals may be instituted only by the defendant. Involves a retrial of the case.

HIGH COURT OF JUSTICE

Chancery Division Lord Chancellor (nominally) and 67 judges Cases formerly in field of equity like estates or bankruptcy.	**Probate, Divorce, and Admiralty Division** President and 11 judges Wills, divorces, maritime cases.
Queen's Bench Division Lord Chief Justice and 35 judges Any Civil case.	**Court of Assize** 1 judge of Queen's Bench Serious offenses including murder and treason.

Lower Courts 79 county court judges About 400 county courts Civil cases not exceeding £400.	**Quarter Sessions** Justices of the Peace for a county 98 separate borough quarter-session courts 65 courts of county quarter session Cases like assault, stealing, or house breaking where specialized judicial knowledge not essential.

MAGISTRATES COURTS

Juvenile Courts Not more than 3 judges from Petty Sessions Specially constituted. For those under age 17.	**Petty Sessions** 2 or more Justices of the Peace Minor offenses and investigation of cases to be referred to higher court for jury trial.

There are a number of special courts. Coroners' courts are convened when a person appears to have died violently or unnaturally. The Coroner (in Scotland the Procurator-Fiscal), who is a doctor or lawyer appointed by the local authority, holds an inquiry and may hold an inquest in court. There may have to be a jury, except in Scotland.

Outside the ordinary hierarchy of courts are administrative tribunals set up by act of Parliament to exercise judicial or quasi-judicial functions. There are now over 2000 of these and their members are usually appointed by the minister concerned with the subject (the Lord Chancellor appointing legal members). These tribunals vary from important legal bodies like the Transport Tribunal which determines railway passenger fares, and administrative bodies like the Special Commissioners of Income Tax, to Rent Tribunals of laymen who have the power to determine the rents of certain properties. Many lawyers have been disturbed by the proliferation of administrative tribunals and as a result of an inquiry the Tribunals and Inquiries Act of 1958 provided for an appeal on points of law from the more important tribunals to the High Court or at least some other referee.

JUDGES, JURIES, AND MAGISTRATES

When the British speak of the "majesty of the law" they really mean it. Nothing gives a more solemn air to a court than the wigs and gowns of the judges and barristers. Few spectators are unmoved by the sight of the judges in their scarlet proceeding to the local cathedral for the Assize Service for a time of devotion before their often deadly business begins.

Trial by jury occurs at the third and fourth levels in the criminal hierarchy. There is no jury at a magistrate's court since this refers serious offenses to either Quarter Sessions or the Assizes for trial by jury. Nor is there a jury at the Appeal level.

A great amount of work is done by magistrates. In large cities there may be a stipendiary magistrate but the tradition is for unpaid lay magistrates to sit either alone or in petty sessions, aided by a legally trained clerk. There persons are known as justices of the peace and proudly add the letters J.P. after their names, an honor second only to that of MP. Even Quarter Sessions, especially in the counties, are staffed largely by justices of the peace. But many boroughs now have their own Courts of Quarter Sessions presided over by a recorder, a practising barrister who is sole judge.

Criminal prosecutions are usually initiated and conducted by the police. Important indictments, e.g., security cases, are the responsibility of the Director of Public Prosecutions. Civil proceedings are of course a private matter.

Two tendencies are worth noting: One is for trial by jury to be in decline, offenders preferring either summary jurisdiction before a magistrate or trial before a judge. The other is for lay magistrates to be giving way to judges at the Quarter Sessions level. Legal commentators seem to welcome professionalization but agree with the 1948 Royal Commission report (Cmnd. 7463) that to replace lay by stipendiary magistrates would be very expensive and would eliminate a valuable association of laymen with the legal profession. Nevertheless they think that the quality of justice would be improved.

THE INDEPENDENCE OF THE JUDICIARY

It is a truism that an Englishman's home is his castle. This sense of security is in large measure due to the vigilance of English lawyers and the impartiality of the English courts. Yet there are frequent countersuggestions that "justice is open to all, like the Ritz Hotel" and that the judges show a certain class and conservative bias. How are we to reconcile such statements?

There seems to have been a certain confusion in the arguments over the merits of the English legal system, even though they have gone on for centuries. It is necessary to distinguish between four quite distinct points of dispute: the handling of cases; the dependence of the judiciary on the executive for appointment and dismissal; the social bias of judges; and the control of the judiciary by the leading members of the legal profession.

As far as the handling of cases is concerned the British judiciary is free from those political pressures which make justice in Fascist, Communist and dictatorial states subordinate to "reasons of state." For this reason the British have always been proud of their legal system, since it places the individual before the state.

The dependence of the judges on the executive is more formal than real. There are no really political appointments other than that of Lord Chancellor (who is usually a leading barrister) and the sharing of responsibility for appointments between him and the Prime Minister would seem to be a judicious compromise between the interests of the legal profession and those of the general public whom the Government represents.

The problem of social bias in judges is more difficult to resolve. All good judges must to some extent be cut off from the man in the street by the very nature of their training and office. In Britain, however, the problem is made more acute by the custom of recruiting the Bench from the Bar, that is of appointing only barristers (not solicitors) as judges. These people would have lived precarious lives at the start of their careers unless they had private incomes and so the odds are in favor of judges being selected from upper-income groups who have enjoyed a private education. On the other hand the noblesse oblige tradition sometimes tends to make them sympathetic to people in humbler circumstances.

The final criticism, that control of the judicial system is in the hands of the legal establishment, seems valid but unsurprising. In Britain as in many other countries, there is a sort of self-perpetuating estate tradition whereby the great universities and public schools appoint people of their own type, generation after generation. To some extent these institutions reflect the times in which they live, but they may be somewhat out of touch with current developments.

What, then, ought we to conclude from these observations? Simply this: the British judiciary is independent as a legal system interpreting the law: it is dependent on the Crown for the appointment of judges: it tends to have an upper-class social bias in the type of men recruited via the Bar to the Bench; and power seems to lie very much with the legal establishment itself except when the Government by judicious (or injudicious) selection of a Lord Chancellor alters existing arrangements.

THE POLICE AND SECURITY

Order is kept in Britain by 70,000 policemen in the various police forces of the counties and county boroughs and by the 18,000-strong Metropolitan Police (in London). In times of crisis, such as the General Strike of 1926, special constables are enrolled to provide extra strength. Very occasionally the police force is unable to deal with disturbances, e.g., the unrest at the close of World War I, and on these occasions the troops have had to be called in to preserve order. More common is the use of troops to keep the wheels turning when a strike paralyzes a vital sector of industry or commerce. Troops are not used as strike-breakers but as temporary help to prevent dislocation. Emphasis on the rarity of revolution and rioting in Britain must not blind foreign observers to the fact that in the United Kingdom, as everywhere else, social tensions have always existed, and Britain's history, even of the past hundred years, is strewn with incidents which could have erupted into serious conflict.

Today the whole question of order and its preservation is under review. The great robberies of the past few years and the various security cases which have been headlined in the newspapers have made people ask two important questions:

1. Is the local organization of the police adequate to cope with criminals who are mobile, nationally organized and expertly trained?
2. Are the security arrangements of the government adequate to meet the threat of subversion and espionage in an age when large numbers of people have access to classified information and when inevitably some of these have weaknesses of character which are hard to detect and easy to exploit?

The ordinary policeman in Britain, outside London, is a member of a county or county borough police force. Each force is directed by a Chief Constable whose appointment and dismissal is made by the appropriate local authority subject to the approval of the Home Secretary (in England and Wales) or the Secretary of State for Scotland. Standards are maintained through periodic inspection by Her Majesty's Inspectors of Constabulary. The actual operation of the various police forces is not easy to explain because it depends very much on collaboration between the Home Office, the chief constable, and the local authority. The Home Secretary is now assisted by a Chief Inspector of Constabulary and eight inspectors to ensure that standards are maintained, and is empowered to retire a chief constable in the interests of efficiency. The police are carefully controlled by law as well as by government and any departure from the rules is severely dealt with.

It is worth noting that the emphasis on local control does not include the capital city where, of course, there is always the danger of national demonstrations getting out of hand. Neither the London County Council nor the metropolitan boroughs have been given control over the Metropolitan Police. This force is directed by the Home Office through a special Commissioner of the Metropolitan Police whose headquarters are at Scotland Yard.

When a crime is committed outside London, as every detective-story reader knows, the local chief constable sends detectives from his own force. Only if he believes that these are inadequate does he "send for Scotland Yard." In 1963 there were complaints that this delay enabled the perpetrators of England's Great Train Robbery to escape with their haul of $7 million (though some of the robbers were later arrested and sent to prison). The Criminal Investigation Department (CID) of Scotland Yard is of course always the body which investigates crimes in the metropolis.

British policemen are still unarmed. They are not highly paid, and though the "bobbies on the beat" have largely given way to prowl cars the police are not always of adequate caliber to cope with the complexities of modern crime. In the 1930s a Police College was established to cream off future police officers, but there remains a strong feeling that promotion should depend on experience and seniority (though many forces are commanded by Chief Constables who are retired officers in one or other of the armed services). Many people prefer the local organization of the police (in 157 separate forces) as a treasured part of the

"British way of life" but there can be little doubt that if the police prove unable to cope with serious crimes then new methods of organization will be introduced. In 1962 the Royal Commission on the Police recommended a reduction in the number of police forces and greater uniformity in their composition and functions. On the whole the British have resisted the notion of a single organization which if improperly handled could degenerate into a Gestapo or NKVD. But the local organization of forces is not adequate to deal with national crime and the growth of organized gangs of criminals is causing many changes to be undertaken.

"Security" in Britain is handled by various agencies, particularly M.I. 5 (Military Intelligence) and the Special Branch of the Metropolitan Police Force's Criminal Investigation Department. The public's attitude toward security seems to have gone through at least three phases. In the first, which lasted until the end of the Second World War, there was a widespread belief that British intelligence (and presumably counterintelligence) was the best in the world. In the second phase, as a result of the celebrated cases of disloyal scientists and defecting diplomats, there was increasing fear lest McCarthy-type investigations be introduced in Britain, with corresponding intimidation of innocent people. Few persons believed that the security services were inadequate; it was assumed that the spread of communism merely meant the introduction of a new dimension.

The third phase has been one of widespread concern about the competence of those responsible for security arrangements. The Vassall case involving Admiralty secrets and the Profumo affair involving the conduct of the War Ministry undermined public confidence in the Government and civil service. Each time a case has become public knowledge the Government has promised to tighten up procedures.

As early as 1948 civil servants believed to be politically unreliable were removed from "sensitive" posts. In 1956 this was extended to people suspected of being personally unreliable and the reliability of an employee's family became a relevant consideration. Those affected were transferred or allowed to resign without discredit. A few were dismissed. An appeal to an independent committee was permitted. Since a civil servant's position is formally at the pleasure of the Crown (though in practice a permanent one) the whole procedure has had to be informal rather than judicial.

The basic problem of security remains insoluble. No one knows how many young Englishmen (or Americans or even Russians) read subversive literature and are persuaded to adopt an alien creed. No one knows how many of them are ensnared by intelligence agencies and betray their country for a principle they place higher than patriotism. Only when they commit a mistake which is detected are they discovered. Virtually no one today is above suspicion and this is a terrifyingly insecure state of affairs everywhere.

It affects the British more than most people because their system depends on a full and frank sharing of confidence within a certain informal network. The civil service, judiciary, university system, armed forces—all depend on shared values into which the betrayal of one's country never used to enter. A former Labour Cabinet minister could still write in 1956, after the Burgess and Maclean defection from the Foreign Service to the Soviet Union, the following account of someone whom he met:

Our informant looked and talked like a credible witness. Eton, Oxford, the Guards in the War, and the Foreign Service after it, though he had retired from this some years before, were on his record[4]

Nothing could be more devastating for the traditional organic society of Britain than the widespread conviction that such a background no longer provided assurance of a man's integrity.

It used to be said that an Englishman's word was his bond. On this foundation an excellent and elaborate judicial system, copied elsewhere in the Anglo-American world, was established. The rule of law enabled the police to remain unarmed. Cut off from the turmoil of the Continent by the English Channel the British people remained proudly free from foreign invasion and free from the internal oppression of royal tyranny. Their ar-

[4] Hugh Dalton, *The Fateful Years*, London: Frederick Muller, 1957, p. 132.

rangements for the preservation of law and order reflect this enviable ability to govern and be governed without popular panic or legislative inquiries into un-British activities.

But recent events have affected the serenity even of "the sceptr'd isle." The executive branch of government has had to encroach, albeit unwillingly, on treasured liberties, with the result that there is now an extensive array of administrative tribunals, a more centrally controlled police system, and a more careful supervision of the political activities of countless public servants. Britain, like other liberal democracies, is challenged not only from without but from within.

PART III

The Political System: A Pluralistic-Organic Structure

The British political system depends very much on informal understandings as well as on the formal provisions of the Constitution. As we have seen it works as a somewhat mysterious body politic rather than as a carefully contrived mechanism of checks and balances. Like the human body, it has by a process of evolution adapted itself to a changing environment, sloughing off useless elements and developing those attributes which enable it to meet the new demands laid upon it. A hundred years ago Bagehot distinguished between the dignified and efficient institutions of government—between the monarchy and the cabinet. Today we are almost tempted to transfer Parliament itself from the efficient to the dignified group of institutions. The House of Lords has certainly joined the monarchy as part of the dignified body politic; the monarchy and the Lords are parts of the traditional body politic which are in decay.

Bagehot also observed that the Cabinet was the buckle that bound Crown and Parliament: today it is more accurate to think of the House of Commons as the buckle which joins the Cabinet and the people. It is a sounding board for Government policy, but it is hardly the center of power. Whether in fact the parliamentary system will survive the discovery of backbenchers that they are spending their lives as mere auxiliaries in the decision-making process is perhaps questionable, not only in Britain but in other parliamentary countries. Unlike the monarchy and the Lords, the House of Commons is hardly a part of the body politic in decay, but there is reason to suspect that it has long been in decline, particularly if by House of Commons we mean those members not privileged to sit on the front benches.

Since 1689, as the astute John Locke foresaw in his Second Treatise of Civil Government, power has always been divided in England. In a sense it is the Government which has the main power (e.g., to declare war); in a sense it is Parliament which is supreme (for it may refuse the money to prosecute the war); in a very real sense the people are supreme, especially at election time.

Parliamentary supremacy means that between elections the House of Commons—not the people—is responsible for broad policy. The people are not consulted by referenda, and members of Parliament are expected to be representatives, not delegates, from their constituencies.

It also means that the House is ultimately supreme over the Government. Even in the eighteenth century Parliament could insist on the appointment of a Government which had its confidence, not simply the confidence of the monarch. It also meant that the continuation of a Government in office depended upon the Commons' grant of supplies. Thirdly, it meant that the dismissal of the Government could come about at any time the House chose to pass a vote of censure. The decline of the House of Commons is attributed to the decline in importance of each of these three powers.

While it is still true that the Government must have the confidence of Parliament and not the monarch, in practice the Prime Minister acts for the government in making appointments. He must satisfy his party in general, but the party is unable to do much about individual appointments, though it may urge a Prime Minister who no longer has the confidence of the country, the House, or the party, e.g., Mr. Macmillan after the Profumo scandal, to resign.

The continuation of a Government depends on the grant of supplies but despite the time spent by the House of Commons examining estimates, the Government is rarely forced to reduce even one of them. If the Government announces a programme of expenditure, it may be assumed that the money will be voted by Parliament. Cuts in expenditure, as in balance of payments crises, are made by the Government, not by the House of Commons.

Perhaps the most crucial and controversial issue is the power of the House of Commons to dismiss a Government, a power frequently used in what some consider the Golden Age of parliamentary government—the nineteenth century. Where a Government has had a small majority, for example the Labour

Governments of 1951 and 1964, or where there is a minority Government, the last being formed in 1929, then the power of the House to dismiss a Government is very real. But no Government with a sizeable majority has been defeated in the twentieth century.

What does this decline in "parliamentary supremacy" mean? It means that in many ways (as we saw in Chapter Three) a Government is more powerful today than ever before, confident in the support of its disciplined majority. But despite their appearance of overwhelming authority, Governments are still not all-powerful. By no means all the power which has slipped from the grasp of the House has passed to the Prime Minister or Cabinet. Much has passed to the private parliamentary caucus; some has passed to outside pressure groups; and some has passed to public opinion expressed through opinion polls. It is through these informal pressures exerted on the Government that policies are changed, not through votes in the House of Commons.

It is arguable that party caucuses, pressure groups, and public opinion have always been important influences on government. This is true. What has changed has been the way in which they operate. A hundred years ago they would determine the way in which MPs voted and so "division lists" were important. Today pressure is exerted directly on the Government, not through the individual member of the House. Although the House continues to "express the mind of the people" and to "teach the nation what it does not know and to make it hear what otherwise it would not," to quote Bagehot again, interest in the House of Commons seems to have declined, to judge by purchases of the daily record called Hansard. In 1945, 8889 copies were bought daily; in 1950, 3384; and in 1963, 2170. But power has also passed to bodies outside Parliament altogether: to the national party organizations which have grown up in the last half century or more and to the great interest groups—business, professional, and trade union. The political structure of modern Britain has many of the attributes of a pluralist society.

In Part Three we shall describe the nature of this pluralist-organic structure. Parts of the traditional body politic may in

some respects be in decline and parts even in decay, but Britain's
new pluralist society is very much alive. We shall begin with the
House of Commons, the latest part of the body politic to come
under fire from critics.

CHAPTER SIX

The Body Politic in Decline:
The House of Commons

> *If the Government or its officers are to be pulled up in the midst of their administration to be examined on current administration before a committee of Parliament I think it is disturbing, highly inconvenient, and will weaken the efficiency of Whitehall administration.*
>
> Herbert Morrison

THE ABOVE QUOTATION from a former Cabinet minister indicates that the attitude towards the legislature found in Britain is somewhat different from that in the United States. There is no denying the esteem in which men like Morrison and Churchill have held Parliament; but it is not the same respect which observers have detected in the American executive branch in its attitude towards Congress—which still holds the purse strings. Parliament itself, of course, is like Congress only in its formal structure—its bicameralism, division of members according to party, and legislative procedure. Certainly the power of the House of Commons is very different from that of the House of Representatives. And whereas Congress itself is but one branch of government, Parliament is supreme political authority.

Composition

The House of Commons is larger in numbers than the House of Representatives (630 instead of 435) but its chamber is smaller in size. Instead of the customary individual desks arranged in a semicircle, the Commons continues the old tradition established when it met in the Church of St. Stephen's, Westminster. Members sit in the equivalent of pews which face each other across the aisle. These are called benches and the front bench to the right of the Speaker is traditionally reserved for members of the Government. Opposition leaders sit on the opposing front bench—hence the term Opposition—and behind the two groups of leaders the cohorts of backbenchers distribute themselves as best they can. Frontbenchers may put their feet up on the Table and speak from the Despatch Box; backbenchers speak from their place and may find difficulty in catching the Speaker's eye. (The Speaker is presumed by all parties to be completely impartial and above the party battle.) Needless to say, the difference in status is in accordance with the general tenor of British life, and the aim of politically ambitious backbenchers, except for a few gadflies, is to sit on the front bench and to enjoy the many perquisites of ministerial office. Minor opposition parties are put in a quandary because contrary to popular supposition there are no crossbenches and they must choose whether to join the Government or Opposition benches. Fortunately, each side is divided by a "gangway" and the Liberals can sit on the second Opposition bench below the gangway.[1] Speeches are usually short—10 to 20 minutes for backbenchers, 20 to 30 minutes for frontbenchers.

The chamber, then, is small. This is often explained as merely the consequence of tradition, but it is not entirely true. Twice the Commons chamber has had to be rebuilt (a fact which is not too widely known); both after the fire of 1834 and after the bombing in 1945 a decision was taken up to keep the chamber small so that only two-thirds of the 630 members could be seated at any one time. This was done to preserve the intimacy of debate,

[1] The corner seat below the gangway was for many years reserved by convention for Winston Churchill. Before World War II Churchill refused to side with the National Government even though he was a Conservative, but his standing as a former Chancellor of the Exchequer gave him special status even then, and he sat below the gangway in solitary majesty firing his salvoes, often with typical Churchillian ingenuity, sideways.

and of course on great occasions when the place overflows the sense of drama is heightened by the crowding of the aisles and gangways.

By and large British parliamentary government is carried on in the form of a dialogue between two great parties. The most important development has of course been the replacement of the Liberals by the Labour party. Third parties have, however, a great place in modern British political history and it would be wrong to assume that the two-party dialogue carried on since 1945 will go on forever; at any time one of the parties can split on some issue of principle and the tripartite system be recreated. Party lines nowadays tend to be drawn much more sharply than in the nineteenth century. Although occasionally a member actually "moves across the aisle" to become a member of the other party, it is rare for a member to vote with the opposing party. For the most part there is a clear party division and there is very little crossing of party lines in voting on bills. Members of Parliament (known as MPs) need only be 21 years of age and one eighteenth-century MP, William Pitt, became Prime Minister at 24. Members need not reside in or near their constituencies, and this makes it possible for ambitious young London politicians to go down to the country, to be approved by the local selection committee, and to "nurse" a constituency in the hope of ultimately being elected there or elsewhere. Since local districts and regions have so little say in national policy, the pork barrel and logrolling are almost unknown. Decisions are made in government departments in Whitehall and, as Jennings has put it, "the pork barrel is locked up at No. 11 Downing Street" (home of the Chancellor of the Exchequer). Nor is there nowadays any gerrymandering. The Boundary Commission redraws constituency boundaries at frequent intervals without regard for party alignments. This commission, consisting of the Speaker and four senior officials, was set up by a Labour Government which actually suffered at the next election from the redistricting which took place.

It is possible that the seduction of the Labour party by the Conservatives has been so successful that the Left has been persuaded to adopt a code of behavior, e.g., in appointments to senior positions in government service, which tends in many instances to be to the advantage of the more conservative elements in the country. There has been a Labour Speaker of the House of Commons only since 1965.[2]

In composition the House has changed less than the electorate. More members belong to the Church of England than to any other church. Only 20 percent of MPs are lawyers. This is largely because there are other avenues to politics. Until recently MPs were largely drawn from a public-spirited leisure class. The convenience of the City of Westminster to the City of London enables far more businessmen to combine business and politics than is possible in Washington. While the proportion of university educated MPs is lower in the Conservative party than in either of the American parties and lower still in the Labour party, it is worth noting that nearly half the Conservatives were at either Oxford or Cambridge.

The pay of members in the House of Commons has been low by the standards of other advanced countries.[3] The argument against adequate salaries has usually been that these encourage the development of a class of "professional politicians" —though it is difficult to think of those members who have served for twenty years or more as anything else. But MPs enjoy social prestige partly because of their "amateur" status, and many of them successfully combine membership of the House with a business or professional career. The Stock Exchange and Law Courts close at 3 P.M., shortly after Parliament has begun. This works to the advantage of the Conservatives and tends to make the Labour party dependent on members who receive subventions from trade unions or who are able to make a living as journalists or television commentators. The salaried middle class tends to be underrepresented.

[2] Jennings attributes the decline in obstructive tactics by Opposition parties since 1919 to the rise of the Labour party with its firm adherence to the principle of majority rule. If so, it is not surprising that rogue elephant MPs like Bevan felt so frustrated.

[3] Although salaries were raised by the new Labour Government from October 1964, the increase was only from $4900 to $9000—still hardly an adequate middle-class salary for anyone maintaining two homes.

Since about half the members are engaged in their own affairs until the late afternoon the business of committee work falls to the remainder, who often resent doing the hard work while the prima donnas achieve prominence in debate. An American representative obtains prestige through solid work on committees; his British counterpart must catch the eye of the party leaders in the chamber and show a combination of loyalty in his voting record and ability in debate.[4]

Table 6.1. Education, Occupations, and Religion
of MPs Elected in 1964

	Labour	Conservative	Liberal
Education (full time)			
Public school only	99	3	—
High school only	76	36	2
Private ('public') school only	8	73	—
High school and university	86	36	5
Private school and university	48	156	2
Total MPs	317	304	9
Eton College (a 'public' school)	2	68	2
Oxford University	41	92	3
Cambridge University	19	67	1
Occupations			
Professions	128	146	5
Business	34	80	2
Miscellaneous (farmers, journalists, etc.)	52	75	2
Workers	103	2	—
Religion (other than Church of England)			
Roman Catholic	17	15	—
Jew	30	2	—
Nonconformist	47	6	1

SOURCE: Data from D. E. Butler and Anthony King, *The British General Election of 1964*, New York: Macmillan, 1965, pp. 235, 237, 238.

[4] In 1957 John Kennedy was given a place on the Senate Foreign Relations Committee instead of the more senior Kefauver. It was said that Kefauver had conducted highly publicized investigations while Kennedy had been tending to the routine jobs of a Senator.

POWERS

The House of Commons has several important functions. It helps to make laws and as the sole source of finance it legislates in money matters. It controls the Government through motions and questions. By custom it is consulted before the ratification of major international agreements, although the conduct of foreign policy is a royal prerogative exercised in fact by the Government.

The power of the House of Commons—if we mean by this the whole House including the Government—is of course overwhelming, as the monarch and the House of Lords have discovered. Unlike the House of Representatives, it does not have to stand by while its proposals are mutilated by the Senate and vetoed by the President. Its legislation, once passed, tends to be modified only slightly by the House of Lords; and the House of Commons can, if it chooses, reject the Lords' amendments to bills as a result of the Parliament Acts of 1911 and 1949. This also means that in financial matters the Commons not only initiates debate: it is, formally, supreme authority.[5] The battles fought in the seventeenth century were not fought in vain, at least so far as outside interference was concerned. (Whether it is the Commons or the Cabinet which really controls financial policy is another matter.)

Perhaps the most distinctive features of the Commons is its power as a body. Whereas many other legislative bodies entrust matters to committees which then report to the whole house, the Commons insists on debating the principles of each bill at the second reading. (The first reading is the formal introduction of the bill.) Most bills are sponsored by the Government of the day, and it is the debate on the second reading, where Government and Opposition marshal opposing speakers, which is the grand forum of the nation and gives every citizen who is interested a sense of participation. It may be preceded and followed

---

[5] It was stated by Henry IV as long ago as 1407 that "the historical roots of Parliament lie, very simply, in money," and that subsidies were granted by the Commons and assented to by the Lords.

by newspaper editorials and correspondence. Though the vote is usually a foregone conclusion the debate enables everyone to examine the issues and compels the Government in particular to think hard and long about the proposals it will make. The Opposition knows that if it scores a good point it will be able to urge modification of the bill at the committee stage. (A defeat of an important bill at the second reading would be the equivalent of a vote of censure on the Government, which might then resign. The last majority Government to be ejected by vote of the House was the Liberal Government in 1895.)

The unique role of the second reading in British-style parliamentary government is worth noting. The British assume that it is a method far superior to any alternative procedure since it states the issues clearly, and enables the principle of a proposal to be agreed on before a committee gets bogged down in detail. It also prevents a committee from changing the basic structure of the bill. Certainly the procedure enables informed newspaper readers to feel they know what is going on.

On the other hand, it is questionable whether broad principles can be so easily separated from detail. Often the full implications of a proposal become apparent only after long and intricate investigations. Since the main decision is put in the hands of leading politicians who are tempted to reduce technical problems to ideological debating points the weightiest problems of the Welfare State or nationalization may never be given proper investigation. Running through much British public life is a belief in the amateur and distrust of the professional, and the assumption that any problem, however difficult, can be reduced by clever men to simple terms which can be grasped by everyone in a second-reading debate. Jennings seems to condemn the system with his remark that an MP "requires a peculiar type of mind—the sort which enjoys undergraduate debates." And, as many a Rhodes Scholar has discovered at Oxford, English undergraduate debates often lack the seriousness of purpose, attention to detail and knowledge of the facts which foreigners take for granted. (Though, of course, like House of Commons debates they are much more fun, and at their best produce flights of oratory of an excellent quality.)

Two things seem to have prevented the growth of specialized parliamentary committees with adequate research staffs. One is the profound belief held by many backbenchers that the main issues at least should be discussed openly by Parliament as a whole, not in the semisecret committee rooms where all sorts of pressures can be applied. The Commons chamber is, as it were, the guardian of the public interest.

The other is that ministers find that the system helps them to secure the passage of legislation, since they are not balked by standing committees which have acquired expert knowledge of their own. There is no evidence that committees ever bottled up a government bill, and it is doubtful whether they have the power to do so. The Government can almost invariably rely on its majority to pass any provision and to reject any amendment if it insists. If necessary it can cut off debate by what is called the guillotine procedure, that is to say the use of closure to allot a certain time to each part of a bill. No Government has been defeated by a split within the party since 1886. By combining democratic idealism and political realism governments have been able to preserve traditional practices. These may be changed if the British people and their representatives cease to take full-dress debates as serious attempts to discern the public interest and if the House of Commons (including the Government!) feels that governmental power needs to be curbed by a more specialized and powerful committee system.

The Business of the House of Commons

The most significant feature of the House of Commons is that it is not simply a legislature, introducing its own bills which become law once approval elsewhere is obtained. For unlike the United States Congress which is mainly a legislative body, chiefly concerned with bills, the House itself is concerned with three different types of business: Questions, Motions, and Bills (including financial legislation). Questions and motions take up about a third of the time of the House. Each of these main areas of business can be subdivided.

QUESTIONS

Questions which take up the hour called Question Time on weekdays except Fridays are submitted in advance by private members, and the appropriate minister may, unless specifically requested, give a written reply. Questions which demand an oral response may be cleverly devised so that a supplementary question can be asked which has not been submitted in advance and which may trap the minister. Senior civil servants spend a lot of time preparing the answers to questions and trying to provide enough information to enable the minister to avoid making a fool of himself. He can always refuse to reply, but if he does this too often or too brazenly there will be Opposition cries of "Answer! Answer!" and the House soon distinguishes ministers whose judgment it can trust from those who are incompetent.

In practice ministers are rarely caught napping because they usually have an apprenticeship as Parliamentary Secretaries (junior ministers) and those who show the requisite qualities are promoted. Political life in the House of Commons is as rough as the infighting in a large corporation, and the apparent gentility of manners in the House should not deceive people into thinking that the largest empire the world has ever seen was created in a fit of absence of mind over strawberries and cream on Westminster's famous Terrace. Question Time is defended as being one of the devices adopted in the House of Commons to keep ministers and their departments on their toes, but some critics think its value is exaggerated.

MOTIONS

Many of the greatest debates in the House have taken place over motions. These are made by the Government or Opposition to enable general debate to take place, for example on foreign affairs, where legislation is rarely involved but policy has to take account of the feeling of the House. Such motions lead to what are called full-dress debates, which may take a day or more. Other motions may be used by the Opposition or private members for smaller but often quite important debates; for example, the debate on the Ferranti Bloodhound missile contract in 1964. Or again, a member may be dissatisfied with the answer he receives to a question and may demand a debate at the earliest opportunity. The Speaker has power to rule whether the matter falls within this rubric and if he agrees a spirited debate may occur in one of these periods which the House allots for the debate of important issues. Each evening there is a motion to adjourn, and this provides the opportunity for half an hour's debate should enough members be anxious to become so engaged. Ten Fridays each session are set apart for private members' motions.

BILLS

In Britain there are two main types of bills, public bills and private bills (though some are "hybrid" bills).

Public bills are divided into two sorts: Government-sponsored bills and private members' bills. Most of the time is taken up by the former and there are complaints that the private member does not have enough opportunity to introduce legislation—being allowed for this purpose only ten short end-of-week sessions on Fridays when many members have gone home for the weekend. One cannot help feeling that the backbenchers could change this situation if they had a good enough case. The fact is that most legislation must be sponsored by Government departments.

It is worth noting the important distinction between private bills and public (including private members') bills. Private bills form a distinct category usually promoted by special interests, such as local authorities wishing to enlarge their boundaries, and are sent to private bill committees—sometimes in the Lords—where counsel represent the parties concerned. Certain legal firms specialize in this form of advocacy and unless a bill is opposed the whole question is dealt with out of the light of public controversy.

Private bills nowadays tend to be comparatively uncontroversial proposals providing benefits or powers not conferred by the law of the land. If they are opposed in any way then they are in for trouble. In the Commons a private bill committee of four MPs will examine the proposal very carefully and even if the bill is finally approved there is the possibility of debate in both Houses. Usually, however, changes are made in committee and Parliament accepts them.

Before we discuss the procedure of the House we should perhaps restate the nature of its business in the light of the foregoing analysis.

Table 6.2. Business of the House of Commons

---

1. *Types of Business*
   - Questions: 1. a. Submitted in advance for written reply
      - b. Submitted in advance for verbal reply
      - 2. Not submitted in advance; for verbal reply (i.e., Supplementary Questions)
   - Motions: 1. By Government or Opposition for full-dress debate
      - 2. By Opposition or private members to debate issues of the day, e.g.,
         - a. debate on adjournment
         - b. debate on definite matters of urgent public importance
      - 3. By Government or private member introducing a bill
   - Bills: 1. Public Bills
      - a. introduced by Government
      - b. introduced by private members
      - 2. Private bills introduced by outside interests and concerning matters of local concern

2. *Value of Procedure*
   - Questions: criticism and defense of Government administration
   - Motions: criticism and defense of Government administration; debate on general principles and policy
   - Bills: debate on general principles and policy; passage of legislation

---

LEGISLATIVE PROCEDURE

As in other countries, bills are introduced formally by having their titles read out. This constitutes the first reading, the first of five or six stages in the House of Commons. But whereas in the United States the next stage is the committee stage—at which point a bill may die a sharp death by being sent to a "killer" committee—in Britain the House proceeds to second reading, a debate on the general principles of the bill.

It is this second reading which, as we have seen, helps to give the House of Commons its unique character, since there is often a crowded debate with leaders of the two parties opening and closing the debate. Next morning the interested educated elite throughout the country follows the debate on the inside pages of *The Times, The Guardian,* or *The Daily Telegraph.* The popular press may provide its own sensational version. In Britain the sense of being a participant in a dramatic dialogue is available to all, every day on which Parliament is sitting.

After second reading, the third stage (omitted if expenditure is not incurred) is the financial resolution of the committee of the whole House. Next there is the committee (the fourth) stage where the details of the bill are hammered out. There is no question now of throwing the bill out and so those who are unhappy about, say, the nationalization of the railways, must use all their ingenuity to rescue what they can from their defeat at second reading by a series of amendments. Here, as in the later stages of the bill, the Government usually manages to prevent complete obstruction by the use of rules introduced in the 1880s when the Irish Nationalists tried to stop the business of the House. Amendments may be selected by the Speaker (the "kangaroo" procedure): debate may be shortened by the House allocating a certain time to each part of the bill (the "guillotine"). Efforts are made to achieve consensus or at least a general sense that matters have been fully discussed and that there has been fair play by having a full debate on the allocation of time motion, even if the Opposition as usual goes down to defeat. (For in the British context, where the Government usually has a reliable majority, some such agreement is necessary if the democratic spirit of give and take is to be meaningful.)

The fifth stage of the bill is the report stage. The House considers the amended bill stage by stage and the minister in charge of the bill offers his own amendments in the light of committee discussion. (If a bill has been referred to the committee of the whole and there are no amendments, the report stage is omitted.) Finally there is the third reading, when another general debate takes place on the amended bill. This may or may not be an important debate, depending on the amount of controversy generated. Many bills, it must be remembered, are relatively uncontroversial: some are very controversial (e.g., nationalization proposals); many are complicated and require earnest and technical consideration. Some bills are withdrawn because of the hostility they arouse (i.e., they displease the Government's back-benchers as well as the Opposition and the public). Those which survive tend in outline at least to be much as the Government originally intended. Mutilation, thanks to party discipline even at the committee stage, is as rare as total destruction. Finally the bill goes to the Lords, after which there may be consideration of the Lords' amendments, and then it receives the royal assent.

Table 6.3.   The Stages of a Bill

House of Commons
1. First reading (A formality)
2. Second reading (An important general debate)
3. Financial resolution in Committee of the Whole (This stage takes place only when money is required.)
4. Committee stage (Bill considered in detail)
5. Report stage (House considers committee amendments)
6. Third reading (Limited general debate)

House of Lords
1 – 6 repeated, except 3

Final Stages
1. Consideration of Lords' amendments (Interchange of messages)
2. Royal Assent (Bill becomes Act of Parliament.)

How, it may be asked, does the House of Commons find time to debate the general principles of all bills? The answer is quite a simple one: the Government is responsible for most legislation through the Future Legislation Committee of the Cabinet. Each week it negotiates with the Opposition through the Whips. These "usual channels" enable business to be dispatched efficiently, the Government realizing that the Opposition must be given ample time to oppose, and the Opposition recognizing that the Government must be given authority to govern. Both exercise their responsibilities with discretion, and it is usually only when negotiations break down that the House sits all night and tempers become frayed. But even this is a good thing, enabling members to let themselves go occasionally.

The parties may of course be a little too responsible. Since the Opposition knows it will one day govern it is reluctant to hamper its own freedom when the time comes. The two-party system in Britain may therefore have contributed to the growth of strong cabinet government: each party knows it will benefit in due course. For example, only one amendment at second reading is permitted, and it is proposed by the official Opposition only. One much-debated feature of the legislative process has been the increasing tendency to introduce legislation which permits ministers to add more detail in the form of orders. Such "delegated legislation" has many advantages for the Government and economizes Parliament's time. Parliament has set up a Select Committee on Statutory Instruments (1944) to examine all new orders and draw the attention of the House to those of which it disapproves.

Committees

The various committees of the House are sufficiently different from those of Congress, and are sufficiently important, to merit separate attention. There are three main types:

Committees of the Whole: financial and legislative
Standing committees: legislative
Select committees: investigation of specific matters

Appointment of committee chairmen is left in the hands of the Speaker who nominates a chairmen's Panel of 10 or more experienced members each session as temporary chairmen of committees of the whole house and as regular chairmen of standing committees.

Like the House of Representatives, the House of Commons can go into committee of the whole at any time it feels that a less formal debate is required. The Speaker leaves his Chair, the mace is removed, and the Chairman (who is also the Deputy Speaker) presides. This committee is always used for the budget, because it is a tradition of the House of Commons that in principle at least every member is directly interested in financial questions. Taxation is decided in the House sitting as the Committee of Ways and Means; expenditure by the House as Committee of Supply. These "committees" are particularly busy between the introduction of the budget in early April and the end of the session about July. The Committee of the Whole—which is the generic term comprising the Committees of Ways and Means and Supply—is also used for bills of first class constitutional importance and for very short or urgent bills.

Unlike legislative committees in most other countries, standing (i.e., legislative) committees of the House of Commons are not specialized. (Indeed they did not exist before 1882.) There is no foreign affairs or judiciary or banking committee, merely new Standing Committees for each bill. Each session 50 members are appointed by the Committee of Selection which consists of 11 senior members representing all parties. (In addition there is also the Scottish Committee which deals with legislation affecting Scotland: all MPs for Scottish constituencies are members. There is also a new Welsh Committee but bills affecting Wales alone are rare.) This means that any standing committee can receive any bill, but there have been complaints that this reduces the expertise of the House and contributes to the power of the Government. In practice the procedure is less amateurish than it looks. In the United States bills go to the specialized committees: in the United Kingdom the specialized members go to the committees dealing with bills which interest them. The minister piloting a bill is a member of the appropriate standing committee: the chairman is drawn from the Speaker's Chairmen's Panel. The Clerk of the House proposed specialized committees in 1945. The Speaker opposed them, saying "You get a collection of cranks, probably, on most subjects."

A standing committee is reduced to considering the details of a bill only; it has no power to send for persons or papers; it has no staff to do research on its behalf; and it merely examines the text of a bill. It has no specialized function and therefore no continuity. British Governments do not have to worry about the line a certain committee has traditionally taken. Since ministers are actually members of committees, as are the Whips, the opportunities for collusion between opposing backbenchers are somewhat rare. However, the chairman of a committee is an arbiter, not a pilot, and may be a member of the Opposition. According to Jennings the Conservative Government after 1951 preferred to take more complex and contentious bills on the floor of the House. The standing committees were under-employed.

If the House wishes to investigate a topic (and occasionally even to discuss a bill) it sets up a select committee (i.e., of investigation), usually of 15 members (which can "send for persons and papers"). Nowadays Governments prefer to do their own investigating or to empower a royal commission, or to appoint a judicial committee of inquiry. No select committee was appointed at the time of the Profumo scandal: the Prime Minister asked Lord Denning, a judge, to make the investigation "after the usual consultations."

Nevertheless select committees have an honorable place in British parliamentary history and four important ones are reappointed annually. These are select committees on:

Public Accounts (established in 1861)
Estimates (1912)
Statutory Instruments (1944)
Nationalized Industries (1956)

The most formidable is the Public Accounts Committee which has the service of one of the few officials still responsible to the

House and not the Crown—the Comptroller and Auditor-General who audits the national accounts. This committee criticizes wasteful expenditure and queries irregularities. Its twin, the Select Committee on Estimates, has until recently had a more difficult task because of lack of staff and inability to question the policy behind the estimates, but appoints sub-committees which inquire into selected ranges of current expenditure with a view to promoting economy and efficiency. The Committee on Statutory Instruments has the assistance of the Speaker's Counsel and is able therefore to pronounce on the legal and constitutional aspects of the orders it reviews. Ministers are compelled to submit these to the committee before they go into law.

The newest of the committees, the Select Committee on Nationalized Industries, was created in 1956 because of a need to submit these great undertakings to more investigation than was possible in the debate on their annual reports to the House of Commons. The committee may concern itself only with those matters for which a minister is responsible but it also pronounces on the operation of the industries as well as obtain useful information about them.[6]

Why, it may be asked, does the House show such decorum and circumspection in its attitude toward the Government? (Its Committee on Procedure even rejected, 8 votes to 6, an experimental specialist committee on colonial affairs in 1959.) Why are there no committees of the sort which in the United States investigate the executive branch and recommend a reduction in the budget? Why should the Government have been able to ban private members' time from 1939 to 1949? What has happened to the great House of Commons of the seventeenth century which challenged the Crown first within the Palace of Westminster and later on the field of battle?

Is it that the House had become the supine slave of the Government? Or is it that the executive in Britain has become so

[6] Reports have been made on the Scottish Electricity Boards (1957), the National Coal Board (1958), the Air Corporations (1959), British Railways (1960), the Gas Industry (1961), and the Electricity Supply Industry (1963).

intertwined with the legislature that instead of the formal checks and balances of the old days (and of the United States today) there are numerous informal conventions? Defenders of the present system argue that any Government which used the power it formally possesses would quickly lose the esteem not only of the Opposition and then the press and public, but of its own backbenchers. They say that it is the combination of willingness to be loyal with a widespread recognition that country comes before party which preserves the democratic character of British politics. They argue that where the exercise of the royal prerogative is in dispute, the House ought not to appoint a select committee. It can, however, address the Crown to appoint a royal commission. The former method is technically an inquiry by Parliament, the latter an inquiry by the Crown; but the result is said to be the same, an examination and public report on the conduct of ministers.

Partisanship in the House of Commons

One of the main criticisms of the political parties is that they demand too much loyalty on the part of their members. Foreign observers are surprised at the apparent docility of British MPs. How do the party Whips manage to keep them so firmly in line—even in opposition when the Whips have no position as Lords of the Treasury, with the access to patronage which this implies? The answer lies in the nature of British politics: people vote for parties, not individuals, and expect party loyalty. A member who "declines the Whip" will have the party's support withdrawn at the next election and most probably will find himself competing against an "officially endorsed" candidate. Nearly always the electorate seems to prefer the official candidate.

Party politics in the British House are both more and less partisan than party politics in Congress. They are less partisan in that nomination of the Speaker is nearly always done by consultation between the parties, and the House has confidence in his nonpartisan behavior once he is elected. Everyone accepts the situation whereby the Prime Minister appoints himself or a senior colleague as Leader of the House (i.e., not only of the majority party) to arrange the business of the chamber. At every stage, however, the Opposition is consulted and the rules of the game are observed. The Leader arranges for debates critical of Government policy by the Opposition. The Opposition must be given every opportunity to oppose: but it must not become an obstruction. Were the Government to lose the confidence of the Opposition that it conformed to the rules of parliamentary give and take, then the latter could degenerate into an obstreperous faction and the whole system would be in jeopardy.[7] For this reason it is most important that members serve an apprenticeship before obtaining ministerial office, and that during this time they acquire an affection and regard for the House itself which transcends party ties. The memoirs of several rebellious members, including those of Aneurin Bevan, testify to the success of the House in stamping so many of its members as "House of Commons men." Observers have drawn attention to the aura which surrounds the office of Mr. Speaker and the great respect shown to him by the Prime Minister and Leader of the Opposition. This is due to the recognition that he stands for the House as a whole—for that sense of the body politic on which parliamentary democracy depends.

On important occasions the Speaker tends to give more debating opportunities to the senior members of each party, but there is rarely a complaint that a member is unable to make himself heard at all. Those who wish to speak have an opportunity to do so, provided they are willing to speak to a virtually empty House. The Opposition has control over the subjects of debate when the House discusses the estimates in Committee of Supply—no less than 26 days being put at its disposal. The Government expects to win every time, but by questioning a particular minister's expenditure (only the Government can propose *additional* expenditure) the Opposition can give a department a very rough time

---

[7] Parnell and the Irish party obstructed the House of Commons. It proved necessary to have a select committee on Standing Orders appointed. Parnell was put on it and behaved as a good parliamentarian!

and provide it with unwelcome publicity. (Of course this is a very far cry from actually reducing a department's budget in the American fashion; in the last analysis British politics seem to be somewhat gentler.) Another example of the less partisan character of British party politics is that despite its patronage the Government frequently appoints members of the Opposition to key jobs in the public service. Thus Alfred Robens, a former Labour minister, became chairman of the National Coal Board and later Lord Robens under the Conservatives. Arm-twisting seems to be less common—though there must be much that goes on behind the scenes in British politics about which the observer can only guess.

In some ways, on the other hand, there is more partisanship in British politics, as we have already seen. There is strict party discipline. There is an underlying ideological conflict between those who support private enterprise and those who prefer the idea of public service. To some extent the postwar ideological battle lines between East and West have been drawn in the parliaments of the Western European democracies, including the House of Commons at Westminster.

In recent years the growth of party solidarity has been sufficiently marked for observers to detect a further element in the political process: the private party meeting in the House. Some have complained that the caucus now determines policy and effectively muzzles recalcitrant members who are forbidden to oppose the party line in public, once they have had their say in private. The Conservatives on the whole have fewer public disciplinary problems than the reform-minded Labour party, but from time to time there are rebellions in both parties when members refuse to accept the party's policy. Some people deplore the discipline which leads to the expulsion of members, but others argue that it is desirable for the party to have a single policy over, say, nuclear arms. The simplest solution might be to have a number of public party caucuses when fundamental issues of policy are discussed. It is disconcerting for the voter not to know whether his member really supports the policy for which he is voting, or to know how divided the party is on an issue. Such public caucuses could take place before the second reading of bills and before important motions were debated in the House.

The Individual MP

Nothing is more often discussed in British political circles than the role of the individual member of Parliament. Have the backbenchers permitted power to pass to the party machines? Has the role of the MP been adapted to meet the needs of a complex society?

In some ways the MP is far less of an individualist than is a congressman. He depends on the support of the party machinery which is based on London. He is not able to vote as he wishes except on such moral issues as Sunday cinemas or licensing hours, when the Whips are withdrawn. He must reconcile himself to the fact that most legislation is Government business.

Yet he remains the individual voter's chief bulwark in distress. Every Englishman knows that when he is in real trouble there is no better advice than "Write to your MP" and often the machinery of state is set in motion (or stopped) so that justice can be done to John Smith. This even extends beyond the boundaries of the United Kingdom. At a time when defeat must have seemed possible during the last war the House spent two days debating whether foreigners in British internment camps were receiving fair treatment.

The main criticism of the present situation is that members of Parliament seem to be increasingly confined to two extremes: general issues of high policy, and comparatively minor details of administration. The House of Commons does not itself sufficiently investigate the great middle ground where so many of the issues are to be found—higher education, nuclear arms, policies of nationalized industries, national security. At international conferences MPs tend to be comparatively uninformed. No committee provides an alternative detailed analysis of problem areas which can be comparable to the Government's White Papers and Blue Books—the official publications on policy.

Yet as we saw in Chapter Four the Government has been found time and again by special commissions of inquiry to have been short-sighted or badly advised in a number of these areas. This suggests that the several hundred members of the House could have spent their time more usefully in committees of inquiry than sitting in the chamber urging on front-bench speakers to higher flights of oratory.

Defenders of the modern House of Commons have had to explain away, if they can, its loss of the power of the purse. The conventional explanation is that such a power is inconsistent with cabinet government. Yet there is something disconcerting about the power of the Treasury—which alone, on one occasion, authorized expenditure in certain colonies above the sum of £150 million appropriated by the House of Commons.

The British have in fact turned the main feature of parliamentary government—control of the executive by the legislature through supply, i.e., financial power—upside down. It is not the House which restrains the Crown but the Crown which restrains the House of Commons. Thus Sir Austen Chamberlain, formerly Chancellor of the Exchequer, could say in 1931 "the more opportunities you give to the House of Commons to discuss Supply the more pressure is put upon Ministers to spend money." Even the Harvard political scientist Professor Beer seems to accept the view that though the financial powers of the British executive "might be thought to be dangerous . . . not the least important safeguard is provided by Treasury control."

At times the House has tried to revert to its former role. During both world wars a Select Committee on National Expenditure was set up by the House of Commons but each was later abandoned. Instead there are the general debates of Government policy on supply days—a poor substitute for detailed accountability and an indication that although it is still a great forum of debate the House of Commons is in decline.

CHAPTER SEVEN

The Body Politic in Decay:
The Monarchy and the
House of Lords

The Monarchy and the Crown

FEW THINGS are more difficult to understand—particularly for a republican—than the concept of the Crown. The formal duties of a President, of whatever nationality, are comparatively easy to explain because they are stated in the Constitution of each country. But nowhere in the documents which form the British Constitution are all the prerogatives of the Crown ever explicitly stated. The rule would seem to be that if clarity is required an act of Parliament is passed. The prerogative remains a vague twilight area of residual powers, some of which, like the treaty power, are considerable.

Why is this so? The answer is not really too complicated. American government assumes that there is something called power which is divisible into the executive, legislative, and judicial branches, each of which is represented by an appropriate institution whose operations are determined by the Constitution.

In a constitutional monarchy the situation is quite different. Originally all the power of the state was vested in the Crown represented by the monarch who was gradually compelled to transfer part of his power to the other bodies, particularly the legislature and judiciary. He also delegated part of it, through royal charters, to local governments, business companies and various public undertakings. Since the eighteenth century monarchies like the British have been described as "constitutional" or "limited." But the fascination of the system lies in the manner in which the monarch has been compelled to dispose of much of his executive power as well. The result is a twofold executive, a powerful Head of Government (usually called Prime Minister) and a relatively powerless Head of State.

Today it is necessary to distinguish the monarch or sovereign from the Crown of which she is but a part. The monarch is a person: the Crown is a symbol—the symbol of supreme executive power. This power used to be wielded by the monarch personally, but in modern constitutional monarchies it is exercised by ministers of the Crown who are still formally the Queen's ministers but who are very much masters in their own house. The archaic style of address used in monarchies may seem more suitable for fairy tales than the modern world of *realpolitik* but we must be tolerant of others' foibles, even if these sometimes seem to make life unnecessarily complicated.

Let us pause for a moment and reflect on the statement that the monarchy is a person while the Crown is a *symbol*. Just what does it mean? The official "explanation" by the British Central Office of Information is that "the Crown vests in the Queen but in general its functions are exercised by Ministers responsible to Parliament. The Queen reigns but does not rule. The United Kingdom is governed by Her Majesty's Government in the name of the Queen." This still does not tell us what the Crown *is*. It is obviously not a sort of hat worn occasionally by the Queen but more often by the Prime Minister. It is more like a seal which is used by the Queen for some functions but by the Prime Minister for a great many more. In other words, there are still some functions belonging to the Crown, i.e., monarch, though most are now the prerogative of the Crown, i.e., Prime Minister (and/or his colleagues in the Cabinet).

In other words, if the monarch as the Crown acted without the advice of a minister she would be acting unconstitutionally; if a minister for his part countersigned a document of which

Parliament disapproved he would lose the confidence of the House and would presumably resign.

Table 7.1. Formal Powers of the Monarch

1. Summoning, proroguing and dissolving Parliament
2. Speech from Throne when Parliament assembles
3. Royal assent to all bills (through Lords Commissioners)
4. Presiding over formal meetings of Privy Council
5. "Fountain of Justice"—pardons
6. "Fountain of Honours"—conferment of honors (except for five Orders to which she appoints members herself)
7. Appointments to important state offices
8. Approval of Cabinet or of individual minister before appointment
9. Temporal head of established Church of England and appointment of leading clerics
10. Concluding treaties and declaring war, making peace and receiving ambassadors

How Exercised

1. By Order in Council (on the advice of the Privy Council)
2. By Order, Commission or Warrant signed by Queen and signed by responsible minister
3. By proclamation, writs, letters patent under Great Seal affixed by Lord Chancellor in obedience to a Royal Warrant signed by a minister.

The monarch has a number of personal prerogatives such as the award of high honors like the Order of Merit. But most are formal political prerogatives no longer exercised personally without the "advice" of the Government. But if a Prime Minister dies or resigns and a successor has to be appointed from the same party, or if there is an inconclusive election in which no party has a majority, the situation is more obscure. The monarch cannot act according to personal preference, if only because the new Prime Minister must have the support of a majority of the House of Commons. Normally, it is true, there is no problem over the appointment of a Premier. Attlee was automatically invited to kiss hands in 1945 after the election, Churchill in 1951, and Wilson in 1964. But when Eden resigned in 1957 it was not clear who was to be his successor until the Queen appointed Macmillan. In 1963 there was similar confusion in the Conservative party until Sir Alec Douglas-Home emerged as the Tories' leader. In 1923 Mr. Baldwin, a commoner, had been selected in preference to Lord Curzon. Nor is it only the Conservatives who get into difficulties. In 1931 King George V invited MacDonald, the Labour Prime Minister, to form a National Government, which he did to the dismay of many of his parliamentary colleagues in the Labour party.

Four appointments in which the monarch has been personally involved in forty years is quite a lot and suggests that the monarch still has a role to play in the most significant of all decisions, the appointment of a Prime Minister. It would therefore seem sensible to consider this prerogative as distinct from both the personal prerogatives and those which are of a formal political kind —such as presiding over meetings of the Privy Council. Yet few British writers are prepared to give this unique personal political prerogative the attention it deserves. For it is generally believed that the monarch does not act without taking the advice of the outgoing Prime Minister and sounding out other party leaders through her private secretaries. But supposing she receives conflicting advice? She is not bound to ask anyone's opinion, and in fact is entitled to consult whom she chooses.

Nobody knows for certain the extent of the monarch's personal influence on the political life of the country. It has been suggested that Attlee took the advice of King George VI in appointing Bevin as Foreign Secretary instead of Dalton. Should we take Attlee's denial at face value? No Labour Premier is likely to admit publicly that the monarch was able to influence his judgment. As for Conservative Prime Ministers, they are brought up to regard loyalty to the monarch as one of the primary virtues and are unlikely ever to tell. No doubt much depends on the good sense of monarch and Premier.

There is still no question of the monarch's right to be consulted, right to encourage, and right to warn. Queen Elizabeth II can expect the Prime Minister to keep her informed, usually by a weekly audience. She can be in touch with other ministers and senior diplomats, directly or indirectly. Such an influence may be negligible—or considerable. Given a conscientious monarch —and with the possible exceptions of Edward VII and Edward VIII all since 1837 have been conscientious—ministers begin to find that there is here a reservoir of experience and simple sagacity which ought not to be ignored. The Prime Minister, surrounded by colleagues jockeying for position, is able to turn to the monarch for some dispassionate observations. One may guess that whereas Churchill did not need the advice of the youthful Queen Elizabeth, today's stripling who is to be Prime Minister thirty years hence assuredly will, if only to draw indirectly upon the experience of his predecessors. And at this point the monarch may become of greater importance than today, for the Queen may acquire an intimate knowledge of men and affairs and have quite an interest in the appointment of, say, a Lord Chief Justice or an Archbishop of Canterbury. We know Queen Victoria could blackball a co-respondent like Sir Charles Dilke from the Cabinet: we do not know if monarchs are able to blackball any appointments today. We know that Queen Victoria intervened on a number of occasions, sometimes successfully: we can only guess what could be the implications for the monarchy if Queen Elizabeth were to feel impelled to do likewise in twenty or thirty years' time.

The monarch, then, has a political role: he or she has what are often thought to be only the formal (but may in fact be real) power over appointments, honors and the like, and has genuine personal responsibility for appointing the Prime Minister and keeping abreast of affairs of state. But in addition the monarch plays an important social role as Head of State. The President of the United States combines the duties of Head of State and Head of Government and manages to avoid too many social functions, particularly those which take him out of the country and even out of Washington, D.C. Members of the royal family have no such inhibitions and regard it as a duty to travel to foreign countries, tour the Commonwealth, and visit every part of the United Kingdom. At times it almost seems as though the British people are in need of this constant attention to keep up their spirits and self-esteem. The House of Commons

Select Committee on the Civil List reported in 1952 that there was an ever-increasing demand for royal visits to various parts of the country for public functions which apparently "give great pleasure to the people and form a most important part of the royal duties." Here we can see how very different a monarchy is from a republic. In the Commonwealth too, people are conscious of the fact that a Governor General or Lieutenant Governor is "the Queen's representative" and must behave accordingly: he is not the servant of the people like the Governor in an American state.

How expensive is the monarchy? By British standards it is considered a bargain: the monarchy is given an annual parliamentary grant of about $1.5 million a year out of which the whole entourage must be paid. (The President of the United States receives less than $700,000 and has 77 servants in the White House.) In return the Exchequer receives a net revenue from the Crown Estate of over $6 million. The Duke of Edinburgh receives as large an income as the President of the United States —about $100,000 a year, and the Prince of Wales $30,000 until he becomes of age (when he will be entitled to the whole revenue from the Duchy of Cornwall—over $250,000 a year). The royal family would not be able to live in style if they did not have a stylish income, much of it from private sources. Few people begrudge them their fine clothes; once they publicized the wealth of the nation, while today they symbolize the determination of the British people to keep up the old standards. Some Americans have criticized the monarchy as an extravagance. But the Queen's household has, on the whole, tended to set a good example in economy (even to the extent until recently of paying lower wages than other employers!).

The main criticism of the monarch is that she still lives the routine life—Buckingham Palace, Balmoral, Sandringham, and Windsor—of an earlier era, with the Queen as fond of horses and as uninterested in the arts as her Hanoverian ancestors. Yet the Duke of Edinburgh and Lord Snowdon have brought some fresh air into the narrow confines of royal family life and certain male relatives of the Queen have married commoners. It is hard to see how the British monarchy can "adapt" itself successfully to a different world. If it becomes Scandinavian and democratic it loses the fairy-tale imperial grandeur which some think alone sustains it in the minds of the British people. If it remains aloof it may comfort the nostalgic for a while, but if Britain fails to adapt herself quickly enough to a rapidly changing world the monarchy may one day be held partly to blame. It would be rash to predict a republican Britain in the present century, but if Queen Elizabeth survives until the 1990s, and particularly if her consort predeceases her, it is possible that the glow of the 1953 Coronation will give place to a certain irritability. The very success of the monarchy in the troubled years since 1945 could be its ultimate downfall.

Two questions remain: In what circumstances might the personal political prerogative be extended? And how can it be circumscribed? As far as extension is concerned, this would be most likely to happen if the two-party system were to disintegrate, and particularly if a multi-party system (even three large parties) were to replace the present rather simply two-party division. For then the choice of Prime Minister could become more open: the monarch would be able to choose a leader from a different party as well as possibly from various candidates from within a party.

How can the prerogative be curtailed? It is really quite simple. The Cabinet or Parliament has only to decide that the monarch should no longer be allowed to exercise a certain prerogative and it can be taken over. The great battles of the seventeenth century were over the extent of the royal prerogative; and the monarch lost. Historically and constitutionally the monarch has usually been in the right when defending his prerogative: but in terms of practical politics and modern democratic theory he is easily put in the wrong and is almost helpless against his twin adversaries—popular feeling and the political power of the politicians. His prerogative can never be extended (except in the unusual circumstances mentioned in the last paragraph) but it is constantly being whittled away—though this does not mean that the prerogative itself is less significant. For modern Cabinets find the Crown's prerogative singularly useful to them and frequently hide behind it when defending themselves in the Commons.

In this section we have tried to avoid the historical development of (or more properly the decline in), the powers of the monarch, though it is as fascinating a way to study British government as, say, the extension of civil rights is for anyone anxious to understand American government. We should however remark that the last exercise of the royal veto in the United Kingdom was in 1707. The British monarch today lacks power: instead there is that elusive attribute called influence.

One final point should be noted. Although no one since the seventeenth century has believed in the divine right of kings it is still true that *in law* the monarch can do no wrong. The Crown can be sued but not the monarch. A moment's reflecton will show that this is a necessary feature of the system. But the monarch for his part must abide by the rules—over which he has little control. If he disobeys he may possibly lose his head (as in 1649) but more likely lose his throne (as in 1688 and 1936).

The House of Lords: A British Senate?

At first glance, the House of Lords would seem to be the British form of the American Senate since both are the upper houses in a bicameral legislature. Indeed a favorite examination question used to ask to what extent the two bodies were alike. Certainly they have much in common, both in what they are and in what they do.

SIMILARITIES

As for what the two bodies are, each traditionally has great prestige as an upper chamber. Each has the comparatively cozy atmosphere of a smallish debating society in which usually less than a hundred members take part; and neither chamber seems to like elaborate rules of procedure, curtailment on the time allowed to members to speak or the use of whips to ensure a favorable vote. The American Senate has never outlawed the filibuster: the House of Lords often closes its debates without a vote.

Nor is this all. Whereas the lower houses must submit to periodic re-election of the whole membership, this does not happen to the upper houses, though the American is replaced gradually, one third every two years. Some people imagine that the House of Lords consists entirely of hereditary peers, but this is not so: the life peers (and peeresses) since 1958, the law lords (since 1876), and the bishops will not hand down their titles. But once made peers they are ennobled for life—unless they choose to renounce their peerage under the 1963 Act. Members of both the Senate and the House of Lords tend to be free from financial worry, either because they are well paid, as in the Senate, or because they tend to belong to the moneyed class as in the House of Lords. In a sense then neither is truly representative of the people as a whole, though of course the Lords are not really representative of anyone. Each has roots in a rural society which is now less influential than the composition of the upper houses would seem to indicate.

The two houses tend to be somewhat conservative in outlook, the traditional prerogative of upper chambers whose duty it has always been to revise and review the work of the more "popular" house. Their members like to think that they are less easily swayed by the passion of the moment—though they tend from time to time to be disturbed by turbulent passions of their own—and they can claim in truth to represent an elite opinion in times of national crisis.

Even in what they do and don't do, the houses have much in common. In the grand tradition of British parliamentary government neither may originate money bills; each can decline to act on proposals emanating from below; and both are the court before which, in extraordinary circumstances, the executive may be impeached by the lower house. (Impeachment died out in England in the late eighteenth century and was always of the ministers of the Crown, not the monarch himself: the only impeachment of a President in the United States was of Andrew Johnson in 1868.)

DIFFERENCES

But these similarities are relatively unimportant compared to the many differences. These can be briefly summarized by saying that whereas the Senate's prestige has increased as the power of the United States has strengthened, the power of the House of Lords has declined even more than the prestige of the United Kingdom. So severe has been the decline of the Lords that the term "Parliament" is now used synonymously with "House of Commons"—the House of Lords becoming an anachronism. Whereas the Senate represents the states of the Union, the Lords mostly "represent" themselves and owe their position to hereditary title or Crown appointment. In a democratic age, aristocracy has but little place. Indeed peers are now entitled to an allowance—$15 for every day they attend debates—an indication of more straitened circumstances, at least of some members. The hereditary peers tend to form a separate caste, cut off from the normal run of people by their titles and coats of arms and the deference which is humbly offered to them and graciously received. Their view of society tends to be somewhat narrow and restricted and it has been this more than anything else which has caused the convention since 1923 that a Prime Minister must be a commoner. Hence the disnoblement of Lord Home before kissing hands as premier in 1963.

COMPOSITION

There are various kinds of peers among the 900 or so entitled to sit in the upper house. Over 800 are hereditary peers (including princes of royal blood) some of whom are of ancient lineage like the Marquis of Salisbury and the Duke of Norfolk (British titles, in order of precedence being Duke, Marquess, Earl, Viscount, Baron—all except Dukes being commonly addressed as "Lord"). But half the peers have titles created in the present century "for services to the nation," often as MPs. Their political services have at times included contributing to the treasury of the party in power, but since the 1920s trafficking in honors has apparently declined and there would be a public outcry if such "political" services significantly outweighed "public" services. It is a tribute to their lordships that public opinion should still regard honors as the reward of *honorable* conduct.

The remaining peers, who seem likely to increase in number, are life peers of one sort or another: the two Anglican Archbishops and 24 of the bishops (the Lords spiritual); the nine Law Lords who by convention form the highest court in the land —comparable in some ways to the United States Supreme Court (though note the apparent confusion of the legislative and judicial powers in Britain); and (most important) the life peers, both male and female, ennobled under the Life Peerages Act of 1958.

These 900 persons, of whom little more than 100 are active in politics, form "the Lords spiritual and temporal"; they include generals like Lord Montgomery, descendants of such great military figures as the Duke of Marlborough, statesmen like Lords Attlee and Avon (Sir Anthony Eden) and a number of trade unionists and professors. If there is any trend it is towards the recognition of public service of a nonmilitary, nonfinancial, and even nonpolitical kind. But it is obvious why the "Establishment" means something in Great Britain—as though Rockefeller, Meany, Robert Frost, Harriman, J. Edgar Hoover, Acheson, Truman, Eisenhower, Bradley, Norstad, and Earl Warren were in the upper house. There is much to be said for a more "democratic" second chamber; but whether the House of Lords can really avoid being fundamentally aristocratic and conservative is somewhat doubtful. The children of Labour peers, such being the nature of British society and its subtle aristocratic embrace, tend to become Conservative; only if life peers come to outnumber the (active) hereditary peers will it be possible for the House to adopt a different style.

FUNCTIONS

The nature of the business of the House of Lords is in principle similar to that of the Commons: questions, motions, and bills. There are fewer rules governing procedure and in general business is conducted informally. The Lords may initiate legislation, though there is the formal rule that Supply bills must originate in the Commons and the convention that important legislation should first be introduced in the lower house.

But essentially the House is a revising chamber. It performs this function in three ways. Most difficult to assess, and yet perhaps most important of all, is its function as an influence. Like the monarch, the House of Lords has the right to encourage, to advise and to warn the Government of the day, through questions in the House, general debates, representation of the Lords in the Cabinet, and informal contacts at Westminster. In the first few days of the session which reconvened in January 1966 the following subjects were debated.

Mass medication (fluoridation of water)
Technical assistance to developing countries
The British Travel Association
The British Film Industry
The Abortion bill
The Veterinary Surgeons bill.
An Order entitled Salmon and Migratory Trout
  (Prohibition of Drift-Net Fishing) (Extension)
  1965 was approved.

A senior Labour Cabinet minister has asserted that no Government studiously and systematically ignores the opinion of the House of Lords. It is an influential body.

In the second place, the House of Lords modifies legislation. In 1947, according to S. E. Finer, 86 amendments to the Transport Bill, one of the great acts of nationalization, were introduced by the Government and another 91 by the Conservative Opposition in the House of Lords. Altogether 450 amendments were discussed and 210 were passed in the Lords—no mean feat for a revising chamber. The Government is not responsible to the Lords but traditionally expects the House to examine bills with more care and leisure than is usually possible in the busy lower house. Very often, amendments made in the Lords are government amendments, and those to which the Government is firmly opposed are unlikely to survive.

The third function of the House of Lords is the most controversial: the rejection of bills. While there is widespread agreement that the Lords may influence and revise legislation, there are many people who think that the Lords should not oppose "the will of the people" as expressed by the Commons. In the past hundreds of "backwoodsmen" have appeared at Westminster to oppose legislation affecting their interests.

In 1909, the Liberal Chancellor of the Exchequer, Lloyd George, introduced a budget which threatened to tax land so severely that the Lords regarded it as a direct attack upon themselves and their property, and indirectly therefore on the upper house. But in rejecting the budget they flouted the convention that taxation was the prerogative of the Commons and in 1911, after two elections in 1910 and the threat of the Government to ask the King (who could not refuse) to create sufficient peers to ensure its victory, the Lords reluctantly passed the Parliament Act which drastically and statutorily reduced the powers of the Lords. Gladstone had thundered a generation earlier that the House of Lords should be ended or mended. Now its composition was not mended—but its powers were thought to be very nearly ended. But so successful was the House in hindering some of the nationalization proposals made after 1945 that in 1949 there was a second act by the Labour Government. This was expected to complete the rout of the Lords, by reducing their powers still further.

The Lords no longer possess the right of absolute veto. They may delay bills by refusing to pass them but if passed in two sessions (or a single year) by the House of Commons they automatically become law. (Between 1911 and 1949 the rule was three sessions and/or two years.) Money bills face a much lower hurdle than this: the Lords may delay them for only 30 days. Thus by challenging the House of Commons the House of Lords seems to have sealed its fate.

This is not quite the whole story however. Neither act mentions statutory orders of the Crown, which increasingly form the bulk of the "legislation" which goes through Parliament. The Lords, if pressed, could still refuse to act on some of these. Nor do the acts refer to private bills such as those prescribed by local authorities. Many of these, being of a semijudicial nature, are actually initiated in the Lords. And as we have seen the acts do not prevent the Lords from debating controversial legislation and influencing public opinion in such a way that the Government may feel bound to modify its stand.

What, then, are we to make of the House of Lords? The best way of looking at it is to regard it par excellence as a cameo of the organically evolutionary style of British politics. On several occasions it has threatened to balk the Commons and cause a first-class constitutional crisis, but each time the House has given way: no revolution has proved necessary. In a miraculous fashion the Lords have managed to retain the affection and respect of the people, despite their opposition to democratic principles, their condescending arrogance, and their pusillanimous weakness when the battle was joined. Other aristocracies have vanished or have been reduced to impotence: only the Lords remain. It is a tribute to their sagacity, and a reflection on the deferential nature of the British people, that they manage to survive.

The dignified functions of the British government—e.g., the Queen's Speech—are carried on in the House of Lords with the parliamentary leaders of the House of Commons standing, with all the humility of men conscious of their power, at the bar of the house. The efficient functions are largely found elsewhere. But the chamber permits the airing of diverse views: offers an honorable form of dismissal to a Prime Minister who wishes to dispose of a friend (or enemy): and socializes the new elite who have made good in one of the newer forms of commerce or industry— the newspaper and beer barons, the motor car viscounts, and so on. A summary of its debates, like those of the House of Commons, is carried in the "quality" newspapers, an indication that the public still takes their Lordships seriously and finds what they say interesting. It is not really surprising that a mild reform of the Lords was undertaken by a Conservative Government. The overwhelming preponderance of Conservatives in the Chamber made it an easy target for the Labour party, and if the House was to retain any influence at all it clearly had to become more lively and more politically viable. By early 1966 over 100 life peerages had been created, the number of divisions when voting took place had increased, and frequently well over 50 members opposed to the Conservative majority were present at debates.

But why, in this democratic age, and despite so many attempts at reform in past decades, has the House not been replaced by a more representative second chamber? The answer is quite simple: most of the Scandinavian countries have adopted a single chamber, and in effect this is what the British have done. No serious reform could avoid increasing the powers of the Lords at the same time as it improved the representative character of the House. No Cabinet and no party in the House of Commons (except for part of the Conservative party) wishes to see the Lords regain power which the Cabinet and House of Commons have been only too happy to secure for themselves. As for the electorate, it is not likely to support the Lords in any campaign against the House of Commons.

There are two extreme positions taken by supporters and opponents of the House of Lords. At the one extreme it is argued that the House of Commons can be partisan and headstrong, especially under a Labour Government, and that the Lords provide a brake. There is some truth in this—and if there were not the Lords would have gone the way of the First Estate in France in 1789 or the Nobles' Estate in Sweden in 1865. In a world where power tends to accompany wealth, the House of Lords still offers prestige to those deserving of honor.[1] Over 200 years ago Montesquieu said that republics stressed the importance of virtue; monarchies that of honor. To this day virtue is as cherished a characteristic in the United States as honor is in the United Kingdom.

As the other extreme there is the view that the Lords are a leftover from a bygone age like the Order of the Garter. Power today lies with the Cabinet, and the smart businessman goes straight to Whitehall where ministers have their offices. And

[1] In the Liberal party's War Council of 1915, only four years after the Parliament Act of 1911, no less than five of the twelve leaders directing the war effort were peers. In 1939, three of the nine members of the Conservative War Cabinet were also peers.

so, according to this view, major reform of the Lords hangs fire. The decision of three leaders in the Lords—Home, Hailsham, and Wedgwood-Benn—to leave it for the Commons has encouraged this more extreme view, which regards the House of Lords as little more than a Government advisory committee.

Most countries distinguish between their modern constitutional period and the previous era, that of the *ancien régime*. Britain does not. The monarchy and the House of Lords still flourish, though shorn of many of their powers. In the past the British have rightly prided themselves on their marvellous capacity for evolution and adaptation, for retaining the form of the old when introducing something new. So long as the sun never set on the British Empire they were admired for their astute combination of the grandeur of Rome and the democratic instincts of the Greeks.

For the English people, as Shakespeare prophetically observed nearly 400 years ago, were a people generously endowed by Providence. To this native good fortune they added the wealth of the Indies, both East and West, and then in the Victorian era became the workshop of the world. Much of the visible architectural legacy of these 400 years bears witness to their taste and to their industry. But how will a people who have grown accustomed to accepting Cicero's dictum that the happy life for a nation is one stable with wealth, rich in resources, spacious with glory and honorable with virtue—how will such a people easily accept the comparatively straitened circumstances which in other empires in history have tended slowly to paralyze initiative? Britain may, like contemporary France and the Netherlands, adapt herself to a new role. The diminution of the role of the Lords in the past sixty years may be an indication that the British retain that shrewd native common sense which enables them to dispense with any institution, whether it be the sixteenth-century Catholic Church or the eighteenth-century House of Stuart or the early twentieth-century Liberal party and the colonial Empire, once they decide it is expedient to do so. On the other hand it is possible that the decay of Britain's ancient institutions, of both monarchy and nobility, may presage a slow disintegration of other elements of the body politic.

Until very recently it was confidently assumed that the British monarchical political structure was organic in the sense that it had evolved (and improved) over the centuries to its present mature form. Two questions are now asked which did not figure largely in earlier discussion, except indirectly in socialist critique. One is whether in addition to change there may also be decay in the system, whether parts of the organism may have become enfeebled as a result of the passage of time and the decline in Britain's power and energy. While it is dangerous to take the analogy with an organism too far and to assume decay to be inevitable, it is foolish to presume that decay and decline are out of the question—or that the British (or anyone else) have evolved a political system which will be eternal.

The second question is whether the evolutionary organic approach to politics is in fact the best. A revolution transforms a society and enables new forces to rise to prominence. In the eighteenth and nineteenth centuries when Britain was still advancing in power, prestige, and prosperity, new social forces were able to emerge and then to control the power structure via the Liberal party and later the Labour party. Britain experienced an industrial rather than a political revolution. But now that her power is waning, her society could become more stagnant and new forces could find it more difficult to make themselves felt. For not only do conservative institutions fight more tenaciously to conserve what they have, once retrenchment becomes the order of the day, but they are less willing than ever to share their diminishing power with other claimants.

However, as we shall see in the next two chapters, there are few indications that Britain's traditional institutions are proving a match for the new pluralistic society which is so evident in modern Britain.

CHAPTER EIGHT

The People and Politics: Elections and Voting Behavior

> *Certain persons are by common consent agreed to be wiser than others, and their opinion is, by consent, to rank for much more than its numerical value. We may in these happy nations weigh votes as well as count them, though in less favoured countries we can count only. But in free nations, the votes so weighed or so counted must decide.*
>
> Walter Bagehot, 1867

GOVERNMENT in the United States surprises Europeans by its obvious dependence on the "will of the people." Politicians make themselves readily available to visitors, and it is a commonplace that policy must not "alienate the voters." College students are important because they are potential voters.

How do we ascertain this "will of the people" in a country like Britain? Clearly we have to ask the people to express their views, and this is done unofficially through opinion polls and officially through elections. But in what sense do they indicate their "will"? Do they vote in their own self-interest, or do they try to act in the public interest? Do they vote as individuals, exercising a rational choice, or do they follow the instructions and even directions of some group—a trade union, ethnic group, a particular religious body, or association of manufacturers? We know a great deal more than we used to about why people behave in politics as they do, particularly in advanced countries like Britain, and though many more inquiries need to be made, we are at least certain that there is no simple explanation. What does seem to be a characteristic of all successful liberal democracies is a certain willingness not to pursue private interests to the point where the national interest (or general consensus) is put in jeopardy.

Three principles seem to have general recognition in Britain. One is that the individual should have the right to voice his opinion and to act alone on at least one occasion, namely election day. Whatever the group pressures, the party line, and the irrational nature of particular votes, the provision of a secret ballot permits everyone, high and low, rich and poor, educated and uneducated, to play a part. Whatever members of an exasperated and exploited proletariat may say about their inability to affect the outcome of elections and the futility of voting, two facts remain.

1. Each vote counts for one: all men are equal.
2. There are more poor people than rich and therefore the former can, if they choose, determine the outcome of an election.

Amid all the Communist talk of economic growth, dynamic leadership, and the uselessness of the "paraphernalia" of liberal democracy, it is worth recalling why our forebears rightly laid such stress on secret elections as the key to democracy.

The second principle is that the will of the people is translated, for practical purposes, as the will of the majority. The majority view is not supposed to be right: indeed it can become the minority viewpoint if opinions change. But it makes more sense to conduct affairs on the basis of what the majority wants than to allow the minority to predominate. If there is an active minority its members must restrain their ardor until they have persuaded a majority to support them. In many countries this is a proposition which impatient activists faced by inertia find difficult to accept. But long experience shows that there is no adequate substitute for majority rule. In Britain this is demonstrated by the acceptance of a two-party system, each party recognizing that for a time at least it must accept minority status.

The third principle is that between elections the electors should have an opportunity to bring pressure to bear on government by acting together in organized groups of their own choosing. These may be political parties which actually contest elections, or they may be groups with narrower interests, e.g., temperance reform or the raising of teachers' salaries. Provided the groups do not interfere with the electoral system or the operation of government they have a proper place in the political process.

It is worth stressing these principles because it is sometimes assumed that the success of liberal democracy depends on some very high-flown principles—the rational estimate of what is in the public interest as this is assessed by the individual in reflective isolation; the existence of a will of the people which is unerringly directed to the public good; the assumption that all groups represent particular private interests which by definition are opposed to the public interest. These extreme "democratic" principles have had more currency in France and America than in Britain where self-interest, the practical value of majority rule, and the necessity for interest groups to have their own niche, have always been understood. It is often said that the British did not recognize the importance of what is now termed the political process until long after the Americans; it would be more correct to say that they took it so much for granted that they did not feel there was anything remarkable to be discovered.

In assessing the role of the public in British politics it is worth noting these two points: that the same general pluralistic principles governing the behavior of individuals, parties, and groups are now accepted in both countries; but that the British have been less ideologically committed to ultrademocratic practices and beliefs than their more revolutionary cousins.

Elections

HOW OFTEN ARE THEY HELD?

Parliamentary elections may take place at any time up to five years after the previous election. Sometimes two occur within a single year: in wartime when the appropriate provisions of the Parliament Act are suspended, elections may not take place at all. There was no election between 1910 and 1918 or between 1935 and 1945. It may seem odd that Parliament is not bound even by such an act as one which determines the frequency of elections, but if this causes surprise, it can only be because the full implications of Parliament's sovereignty have not been grasped. No act of Parliament is more binding than any other. (Of course Parliament is assumed to act in the public interest and not to delay elections unnecessarily.)

The election campaign is only three to six weeks long and there is no nominating process such as precedes the fall American election campaigns. The election is a simple affair, two or more candidates being named on ballot slips which are to be marked with a cross and placed in boxes. Since 1955 there have been 630 constituencies, each of which elects one member, who may be a backbencher or a Cabinet minister. There are 511 constituencies in England, 71 in Scotland, 36 in Wales, and 12 in Northern Ireland. They contain, on the average, 57,000 electors. In law there are no parties and so no party affiliation is stated on the ballot slip; in the House the Speaker replies simply to "the honourable member for Coventry East." One reason for the previously meagre production of scholarly monographs about British parties and groups has been that both lack official status and have until recently been regarded as too amorphous for academic investigation by traditional methods.

WHY ARE ELECTIONS HELD?

It is sometimes said that American elections are being held to bring together 50 disparate parties, while British elections help to indicate that the two parties do differ on certain topics. Certainly there is a general belief in Britain that every now and then it is time for a change, that governments get tired and should be replaced. (No one has satisfactorily explained how the Russian Communists, the Swedish Social Democrats, to say nothing of a number of dictators, have managed to exert their influence for 20 or 30 years.) There is also a fairly widespread belief that a government should ask the people from time to time for a mandate to carry on its policies. This is a twentieth-century notion, which is the British equivalent of popular sovereignty, and means that a government should not introduce legislation of constitutional importance without appealing to the electorate. In 1910, prior to the Parliament Act of 1911, two elections were held, thus confirming the Liberal Government in its belief that it had a popular mandate to restrict the powers of the House of Lords.

Most countries nowadays have elections—of a sort. What distinguishes liberal democracies is the willingness of the leaders of government to stand for election and be defeated if necessary. The 1945 general election in Britain put the popular Churchill out of office, and he accepted his defeat (once he got over the shock!) with typical grace and magnanimity. The unpopular Stalin was never defeated in the rigged Soviet elections.

WHICH PARTY IS USUALLY FAVORED?

No very long periods of single-party ascendancy are discernible in Britain since the Second Reform Bill of 1867. Until World War I the battle was joined between Liberals and Conservatives, though after 1910 the Liberal Government depended on the perilous support of the new Labour party and the Irish Nationalists. Once the wartime coalition (1915–1922) was dissolved British politics entered a state of flux as the Labour party gradually ousted the Liberals. Their minority Governments of 1924 and 1929–1931 were brief so that in retrospect the intervening period seems to have been predominantly Conservative. The year 1945 which brought the Labour Government to power is perhaps the British equivalent of the 1933 New Deal. The Labour party remained in power only from 1945 until 1951. From then on the Conservatives held office until 1964, a remarkable achievement which surprised and then dismayed the younger Labour leaders of the postwar period, eager for power.

In fact, in the 49 years from the formation of the wartime coalition in 1915 to the election of 1964, the Conservatives were in opposition for only 9 years. During the remaining 40 years (i.e., 80 percent of the time) they were either in a governing coalition or were the governing party. Their success was due in large measure to the failure of the Liberal party to come to terms with the new social groups attaining political maturity and responsibility. This failure was originally due to the social divisions which separated middle-class liberals and working-class trade unionists; and was aggravated by the policy of Lloyd George which split the Liberal party in 1922 and led to its disintegration. Later the rising Labour party was unfortunate enough to be in office at the time of the Great Depression and was blamed for Britain's misfortunes. James Ramsay MacDonald, the Labour Prime Minister, allowed the Labour party to be split much as the Liberals under Lloyd George had been a decade earlier: in both cases the Conservatives were the gainers. But whereas the Liberals never recovered, the Labour party gradually regained its strength and was overwhelmingly victorious in 1945.

Why were the Labour party's years of triumph 1945–1951 so short-lived? Partly it was a natural reaction to a very great number of social reforms, comparable in scope to those of the great Liberal Government of 1906–1914. Partly it was because in implementing its programme the Labour party insisted on measures of "austerity," including rationing, which the British hoped would stop with the end of the war. When the Conservatives took office in 1951 they were able to "set the people free" of controls and rationing for the first time in twelve years, and so fortunate were they in doing this just when Britain entered the first boom of the 1950s that they were re-elected in 1955—and again in 1959 after another boom. The conservatives were lucky; however, they deserved much of their success. Immediately after the defeat of 1945 they remodelled their party and prepared to recover their positions as Britain's national governors. Their businessmen and research assistants were lively people in tune with the times. It became fashionable to be a Young Conservative, and in Britain's return to a deferential society the Conservatives were able to exploit their association with the world of glamor, fashion, successful business, Society, and the court.

The odds were therefore stacked against the Labour party throughout the 1950s. Things were not improved by the failure of the party to remodel its organization as well as the Conservatives had done,[1] by the unwillingness of the trade unions to provide the necessary increase in funds—though they were busily obtaining higher wages out of Conservative employers and the Conservative Government—and by the disillusionment of many intellectuals over the apparent bankruptcy of the party in ideas. The party was in no position to sponsor independent and detailed analyses of its creatures, the nationalized industries and the National Health Service. It did not strike the imagination of the public as the party which would refurbish British industry, education, and transport. The memory of austerity lingered on and Labour came to be associated with impractical idealists who could recognize the need to raise old age pensions but were unable to see that the money had to be raised from taxation based on increased productivity. After the election of 1964 the Labour party increased pensions but postponed the necessary increase in taxation. The party won the election largely because of the lack of confidence in the Conservative Government. It obtained fewer votes than in any election since 1945. Under Wilson, the image of the party gradually changed, and by the end of 1965 it was apparent that the Labour Government had its share of competent and realistic administrators. Yet the party fortunately managed to retain much of its traditional idealism.

Late in the 1950s the Liberal party appeared to be staging a comeback, supported by some of the elements of the population which the other parties ignored. But important though the new salaried middle class may be, it has as yet no sense of separate identity comparable to the Conservative party's upper-class image and Labour's blue-collared cohorts. Nevertheless the party doubled its votes in the 1964 election.

WHY DO PEOPLE VOTE THE WAY THEY DO?

There seem to be three main types of investigation into voting behavior. The most old-fashioned, and yet still the most reliable, is to take a look at the election figures and to correlate the num-

[1] Lord Woolton, the Chairman of the Party Organization, was always careful to assure Mr. Morrison, the Labour party's organizer, that in the organization of Transport House the Socialist party had an election machine without parallel.

ber of votes with the number of seats won. In a country like Britain, where single-member constituencies enable a candidate to win in a three-cornered contest even if he does not obtain a majority of the votes cast, still less of the votes on the electoral roll, victory may go to a candidate who merely has a plurality of votes. This may result in a victorious Conservative obtaining 40 percent of the votes and his Labour and Liberal opponents 35 percent and 25 percent each.

What does this mean? Simply this, that whereas a glance at the House of Commons 1915–1964 shows the Conservatives to have been in opposition for only 20 percent of the time, an examination of the voting figures indicates a gradual increase in support for the Labour party over the years—until the election of 1955. Whether the Labour party has passed its peak, like the Liberals before it, or is in temporary difficulties, only the historian can decide, though many pundits have already authoratively pronounced its decline! (See Table 8.1.) Membership of the Labour party so far shows no clear indication of decline, though there seems to have been an end to growth. Individual membership reached its peak in 1950 and trade union membership in 1958.

The other two inquiries go beyond an investigation of election results and seek to answer the question: Why do people vote the way they do? Were anyone to find the answer to this fascinating question he would be most valuable to any political party. And of course should it be discovered that there was a set of conditions then the notion of free, rational, and individual choice would be exploded. We would vote not for the man or party or programme we thought best, i.e., whose election was in the public interest as well as our own, but we would vote without freedom, but according to the type of person we were.

It may well be that the successful party in an election is the one which persuades its own supporters that the opposing party endangers the public interest, while persuading supporters of the opposition party that there is nothing to fear if their party is defeated. In 1959 Mark Abrams carried out a survey which showed that 47 percent of the Conservatives thought that the Labour party *might* "endanger the country's welfare" and of these 16 percent went so far as to say the party *probably would.* But only 28 percent of Labour supporters thought the Conservatives *might* endanger the country's welfare, and a mere 6 percent said it *would.* Of course the Conservatives had the advantage of having been in office for eight years. But there was an ambiguity in the question which Abrams seems not to have detected. Labour respondents may have thought in terms of social welfare—and clearly the Conservatives had not dismantled the Welfare State since obtaining office. Conservative respondents are more likely to have thought in economic and military terms—higher taxes

Table 8.1. Labour Votes 1900–1966

Type of Government	General Election	Labour Votes
Conservative	1900	63,304
Liberal	1906	329,748
Liberal	1910 (Jan.)	511,392
Liberal 1915—Lib. Cons. coalition	1910 (Dec.)	376,581
Liberal-Conservative coalition	1918	2,385,472
Conservative	1922	4,241,383
Labour	1923	4,438,508
Conservative	1924	5,489,077
Labour	1929	8,389,512
Lab. Cons. Lib. *National* coalition	1931	6,649,630
Cons. 1939—Lab. Cons. Lib. Nat. coalition	1935	8,325,491
Labour	1945	11,995,152
Labour	1950	13,266,592
Conservative	1951	13,948,605
Conservative	1955	12,404,970
Conservative	1959	12,215,538
Labour	1964	12,205,814
Labour	1966	13,057,941

for increased social expenditure, opposition to nuclear arms, etc. —and might with some justification feel that in a rather different sense the Labour party might endanger the country's welfare.

In other words one should never assume that people in different parties are arguing about the same issues, and in any case these can quickly change. Opinion surveys are very useful, but while they replace ignorance and speculation with facts, these are sometimes "soft" rather than "hard." Election figures may seem dull because they do not presume to tell us why people voted but they are the hardest of facts (and there is a great difference between giving an opinion to an interviewer and actually voting in an election). Surveys supplement election returns: they certainly have not superseded them.

To the question why people vote the way they do, two types of answer are given.

The first is sociological in the sense that it suggests that people vote in a particular manner because they belong to a certain social class or occupational group. In Britain, as one might expect, the Conservatives were estimated to draw 9 percent of their supporters in 1959 from among the 1.3 million rich and only 5 percent from the 2.8 million poor who by Dr. Gallup's definitions were twice as numerous as the rich. Among the middle classes, as he defined them, the contrast is even more marked, 34 percent of the Conservative vote being drawn from the 6.1 millions in this class, compared with 8 percent of the Labour vote. By contrast the Labour party drew 76 percent of its support from the lower middle and working class who comprised 17.4 million of the 27.6 million voters. But if the Conservatives are so strong in the upper and upper middle classes and the Labour party so strong in the lower and working class, how do the Conservatives win elections? The answer is quite simple. Because of their snob appeal the Conservatives are themselves able to attract a fair proportion of lower-middle and working-class voters—indeed 52 percent of the Conservative electors came from this large group, especially in the new housing areas. It only needs the extra support of the richer classes, who, of course, usually remember to vote to protect their property, and the Conservatives are able to win.

How can we check the accuracy of Gallup's conclusions, based as they are on income qualifications? One is to examine the occupations of electors, as Mark Abrams has done. He reaches much the same conclusion, though his four classes (middle, lower middle, upper working, and lower working) are different from Gallup's and slightly less realistic as Britain becomes an American-style "middle-class" society. The Conservatives were able to attract 35 percent of the upper-working-class voters and 30 percent of the lower-working-class—a remarkable feat considering the Labour party's image as the party of the working man. And so unsuccessful has the Labour party been in attracting the middle classes that even in 1964 it obtained only 28.6 percent of the middle-class and lower-middle-class vote.

Table 8.2.   Voting and Socioeconomic Class, 1959

Group	% of Population	Cons. (%)	Labour (%)	Other (%)
Solid middle class	15	85	10	5
Lower (nonmanual) middle class	20	70	25	5
Upper (manual) working class	30	35	60	5
Solid working class	35	30	65	5

SOURCE: Mark Abrams, data from D. E. Butler & R. Rose, *The British General Election of 1959*, p. 10.

Table 8.3.   Voting and Socioeconomic Class, 1964

Group	% of Population	Conservative (%)	Labour (%)	Liberal (%)	Other (%)
Middle Class	10	74.7	8.9	14.9	1.5
Lower Middle	29	60.7	24.8	13.7	0.8
Skilled working	39	33.9	54.4	10.9	0.8
Unskilled: 'very poor'	31	30.9	59.1	9.1	0.9
Total	100	42.9	44.8	11.4	0.9

SOURCE: Data from D. E. Butler and Anthony King, *The British General Election of 1964*, New York: Macmillan, 1965, p. 296.

None of this is particularly surprising. If the Conservatives win elections, and if the class structure is a pyramid with few rich people and many comparatively poor, then they must be able to attract the support of a large part of the lower layer of the pyramid. Since the 1860s, the Conservative party has devoted attention to the working man's vote, and obviously not without avail. As a party supported by businessmen who (though their opponents fail sometimes to appreciate this) must make a living by successfully assessing the tastes of the consumer, the Conservative party has had an advantage over the Labour party. The latter has been closer to the workers, and yet often further away, if only because yesterday's party activist is today's elder statesman, out of sympathy with young firebrands. The Labour party expels (or repels) some of its young dynamic members; the Conservative opponents are often businessmen who are very much aware of the teenage market—and cater to it.[2]

The other type of answer to the question: Why do people vote as they do? is psychological. That is to say interviewers ask a random sample of the electorate a number of questions and seek to infer from them the reasons (i.e., the motivation) for people voting the way they do. Much of the information obtained has a certain historical interest, but the implicit assumption that one day we can predict the outcome of an election seems unjustified. For example, the explanations of the Eisenhower victories in 1952 and 1956 were of little use when Kennedy was the victorious candidate in 1960. Until 1964, these sorts of inquiries had not been undertaken in Britain because elections are not held at regular intervals and the careful advance planning necessary if complicated questionnaires are to be sent out is peculiarly difficult.

Are there no other reasons for people voting as they do? There are several factors which have not been mentioned in our preoccupation with class and occupation. One has been religion. The poorer Catholics in many cities have been associated with the Labour party, which in Liverpool has been a curious alliance of Roman Catholics and militant Socialist agnostics. Free churchmen, traditionally Liberal, have split between the parties. On the whole nowadays religion is far less important than social class. Another factor is the traditional rural-urban conflict which con-

---

[2] Some Labour writers still assume that the term "middle class" applies primarily to entrepreneurs, not to salaried employees.

tinues even in the homogeneously middle-class United States. The British farmers (half of whom are tenants) have voted for the Conservatives, the party of their landlords. The "burgesses" of the boroughs may today be miners, journalists, or Cooperative-Society officials, but the "knights of the shire" in the counties are still drawn from the same class. A third factor which became apparent in 1959 and 1964 elections was the distinction between the "old" industrial areas, which remained loyal to Labour, and the "new" areas of automobiles, electronics, and light industry which swung more towards the Liberals and Conservatives. (One may hazard the guess that this was not a new discovery, at least to Conservatives: they had long regarded the new towns and cities as likely converts.) Finally, and so far comparatively unimportant, there is the distinction between England, Scotland, Northern Ireland, and Wales. There seems to be little evidence that the people of these countries voted in any way for nationalist reasons. In 1959 the three nationalist parties polled only the following votes.

Scottish Nationalist	21,738
Welsh Nationalist	77,571
Irish Nationalist	63,915
(Sinn Fein)	

It is worth remarking, however, that the Scottish Nationalists polled more votes than they had in any general election since 1945 when they polled 30,594; the Welsh Nationalists polled 14,887 in 1945, 17,680 in 1950, and 45,119 in 1955—which suggests that here is a force which may yet have to be reckoned with. Irish Nationalism, which has been more vehement since the Curragh Mutiny in Ulster in 1913, does not seem to be in such a state. Whereas there were about 150,000 votes in 1945 and 1955, their numbers were much smaller in 1959. Yet in 1964 the Nationalist parties increased their total vote to a record 249,866. But although more candidates were nominated no MPs were elected.

We have not so far mentioned either parties or issues, yet clearly the voters tend to respond when a party succeeds in striking the right note at the right time. The Labour party

seemed the "right" one to many people in 1945. The party therefore thought it had a clear mandate for its postwar legislation.
The Conservatives seemed "right" in 1951 when they claimed
they would end the postwar austerity. As for issues, it is a
common complaint that "nowadays people do not vote on issues
as they used to." In fact they do, as the controversy over nationalization and the Welfare State has indicated. But if a Conservative party offers to retain the social services and to stimulate the
production of consumer goods it effectively blocks its opponents
—until economic growth begins to stagnate. In 1964 the Labour
party accused the Conservatives of so budgeting that a boom,
possibly artificially contrived, occurred before each election, thus
ensuring victory. If so, then the Conservatives made unexpected
use of the weapons of governmental control over the economy
established during the war and maintained by the Labour Government of 1945–1951. Despite foreign fears for the pound
throughout the summer of 1964, as late as October (according to
the Gallup poll) only 24 percent of those interviewed believed
there would be an economic crisis.

In Britain there is a single national campaign between national
parties and the quality of local candidates is considered to be a
secondary consideration. People vote for a party, its platform, and
its leader. They are, in effect, showing preference for one government rather than another. They probably always have—at
least since the repeal of the Corn Laws in 1846. But this trend is
sometimes, like so many others, thought to be a sign of the times,
and of the decay of liberal democracy. (We should remember that
not long ago the newspapers were complaining of the declining
standard of parliamentary debate since the days of Gladstone and
Disraeli—oblivious to the fact that Bevan and Churchill were
providing a creditable alternative.)

What is the Significance of the Electoral System?

The British electoral system allows no place for any device
such as the alternative vote or proportional representation to
promote greater equity in the representation of views. The main

concern is to obtain a simple and clear expression of opinion and if this favors two major parties then, it is argued, so much the better. Political parties which know they are alternative governments take their duties seriously and responsibly, and this is thought to be worth any unfairness which the system imposes on a minority. The British would say that their system permits fair play, even if it does not reflect equity. Thus the Liberals do have an opportunity to present their case, and if it is a good case, so the argument runs, there is no reason why they should not thereby become a major party.

How Expensive Are Elections, and Who Pays for Them?

In Britain elections at the constituency level are not expensive and since the legislation passed by the Labour Government they have been cheap. It costs the candidates little more than $3 million to fight a general election, and in 1959 the average candidate had to find about $2000. Nowadays both parties frown on the demand of local constituencies that candidates shall pay their own way, and independent candidates are rarer than they used to be. Instead the party "machines" seem to supply both candidates and funds. These in turn are furnished less by individuals (it is thought) than by business firms (Conservatives) and trade unions (Labour). Elections are now fought nationally, not locally, and the law does not limit expenditure at this level. Labour headquarters spent nearly $900,000 on advertising alone in the months before the 1964 election. Richard Rose has estimated that the Conservatives and their antinationalization co-campaigners outspent the Labour party in the ratio of nine to one.

We have spoken about the desire of the Labour party to lessen the cost of elections, but this does not mean that either main party favors multiplicity of candidates. The $420 deposit (introduced in 1918) still has to be placed—and forfeited if a candidate obtains less than one-eighth of the poll. This is to stop the nomination of what are called "freak" candidates, a term that illuminates the British approach to politics. The aggressive individualist is frowned on, but only because the British do not like candidates who are irresponsible, the sort of men who never want to form a government but wish merely to be a nuisance. Whether the price now being paid for responsibility—fewer and fewer minor party and independent members—is perhaps a little too high, is often debated.

Four hundred and forty-three deposits were lost in 1950, a record number which cost candidates nearly $200,000; 186 were lost in 1964. This is a deterrent to a new party, or the ever-hopeful Communists. Assuming that 600 candidates in such a party failed to obtain an average of 5,000 votes out of 40,000 cast in each constituency, they would have to pay a total of over $250,000. Few new or small parties have this amount of money to throw away.

Are Elections Fair?

"Unfair" elections fall into various classes. There are those that are rigged by unscrupulous election agents and returning officers —a procedure made virtually impossible by legislation. There are those where universal suffrage is not permitted, a practice ended by the extension of the vote to the urban working men in 1867, the farm laborers in 1884, married women and spinsters over 30 in 1918, and all women as well as all men in 1928. Until recently some British people had two votes, either because they owned property in another constituency or because they were university graduates. Before the 1950 election property owners could have a second vote and 12 MPs were selected by university graduates.

Elections are now fair in Britain in other ways. As we have seen there are strict limits on local election expenses. Before these were restricted, the Conservatives could take advantage of their greater mobility on polling day by the provision of motor transport for voters. (Though many a sound Labour voter used to travel comfortably to the polls in a Conservative car.) Another example of fair play is the registration of voters. Since it occurs annually this means that there is little time lag between eligibility and registration and few potential voters are missed. The government also mails out the basic election material of the parties. The high turnout of British elections is made possible by these arrangements—introduced, like the limitation on election expenses, by the Labour Government in its Representation of the People Act in 1948.

Is there no element of unfairness in British elections other than the curbing of third parties by means of the electoral system of single-member constituencies? In practice there still is some doubt about fair play in parts of Northern Ireland where the Catholic minority, like the Negro minority in the American South, has felt that it is not able to make its voice adequately heard. But the main element of unfairness is of quite an unusual order by American standards: the power of the Prime Minister to dissolve Parliament at any time convenient to him. That this should still exist is the consequence of the monarchical system. Although statutorily, Parliament has ordained that no Parliament shall last more than five years, there has been no limitation of the prerogative which entitles Her Majesty (i.e., the Prime Minister) to dissolve Parliament and call a new one. So useful is this prerogative that it has been annexed by successive Governments as a Crown prerogative and there is no indication that the Labour party will abandon it.

CHAPTER NINE

The New Pluralism:
Parties, Pressure Groups
and Interests of the Realm

The Impact of Pluralism

THE INCREASINGLY pluralistic nature of modern British society
becomes apparent not only from the analysis of elections and
public opinion but from an examination of political parties and
groups. The study of the British political process has been influenced by the explorations of North American political scientists,
and some of these have tended to assume a pluralistic pressure
group framework which sometimes applies more appropriately to
the New World than to the Old.

In his interesting book, *Anatomy of Britain Today* (1965),
Anthony Sampson contrasted the new Britain of manufacturers'
associations, large trade unions and popular newspapers with the
old Britain with its traditional institutions such as the law, the
church, the universities, and the civil service. Implicitly he was
comparing the new pluralism with the old organic structure,
modern pressure groups with traditional "interests of the realm."

For the traditional organic structure of British social (as well
as political) life—sometimes called semifeudal—lingers on. Many
groups are more fittingly described as interests of the realm, an
expression full of Old World charm and dignity. Pressure groups
are modern institutions, private in law and part of the private

175

sector of the economy. They apply pressure on the political system from without. Interests of the realm, less easy to define, are sometimes old (like the City of London) and sometimes new, (like the National Coal Board) and are usually legal entities which can own property, sue and be sued. The more modern interests are usually part of the public sector of the economy. In many instances their senior officials are appointed by the Crown (e.g., board members of nationalized industries, bishops of the Church of England, judges, Oxford Regius professors) or by trustees, and so the institutions are easily identified with what has been termed the Establishment.

Political interest has centered on the pressure groups rather than the interests. For example, the Federation of British Industries, founded in 1916, is a pressure group, a powerful organization of modern business corporations, whereas the corporation of the City of London, an interest of the realm, had already been influential for over a thousand years before it helped to finance the rebellion against King Charles I in the 1640s. Everyone knows that the Federation is a powerful pressure group. Few people pay much attention to the City of London.

Today it is fashionable to dismiss the older interests of the realm as hangovers from the past (and it is in their interest that they should escape investigation!) but the fact remains that it is the City of London which alone resists absorption whenever the boundaries of London are changed, even in 1965 when whole counties were being swallowed up. (William the Conqueror, who built the Tower of London, only gained possession of the city by means of a treaty with the burgesses, granting a charter which is still preserved.) While new pressure groups are constantly coming into being, for example the commercial television lobby of the 1950s, and are becoming the object of scrutiny, it is also true that new organizations more aptly described as interests of the realm have also been established, notably the nationalized industries and the Regional Hospital Boards.

In this chapter we shall discuss separately the political parties, and the chief pressure groups, making some reference to the new interests of the realm.

Political Parties

PARLIAMENTARY PARTIES

Each of the two main parties in 1965 had over 300 MPs. The Liberals had 9. No other party elected an MP.

British parties are famous first and foremost for their party discipline, which involves the use of Whips, the expulsion of recalcitrant members, and the existence of comparatively weak parliamentary committees. Secondly, although each party has wings, one of which has something in common with the nearest wing of their opponents, the parties tend to represent distinct social and ideological groups. No businessman of Conservative views would be at home in the Labour party, while no member of the Fabian Society, a group of intellectually inclined socialists, would be at the same time a Conservative MP. In 1965 all 303 Conservative MPs opposed the nationalization of the steel industry: all but two of the 317 Labour MPs were prepared to support the Government's proposals. Party homogeneity is preserved and encouraged by meetings and party committees. A third important feature of the British parliamentary parties is their role in the selection of party leaders.

The Whips ensure party discipline by issuing "three-line Whips" i.e., requests to members to vote with the party in the form of, for example, *A most important Division will take place and your attendance by 9:30 P.M. is particularly requested*. But their role is not primarily that of disciplinarians. Equally important to seeing that MPs vote (even if they do not attend the preceding debate) is ensuring that the party's leaders keep in touch with the feeling of backbenchers. The Whips also constitute the "usual channels" through which the business of the House is arranged and the Government's weekly programme agreed to by the parties. MPs are expelled only if they consistently refuse 'to accept the Whip," that is to say want to enjoy the privileges of party membership without fulfilling their responsibilities. (An occasional refusal to vote on grounds of conscience may be overlooked.)

The ideological homogeneity of the parties is illustrated by the frequency of party meetings to discuss policy as well as procedure. In the Labour party every MP including the Leader is a member of the parliamentary Labour party and meetings are held at least every two weeks. The party is governed by the Parliamentary Committee of 18 members: the Leader, Deputy Leader, the two Chief Whips, the Chairman of the Peers' Group, 12 elected representatives of MPs and one elected representation of the Labour peers. In opposition this forms the Labour "shadow cabinet"—but of course the composition of the next Labour Government, selected by the Prime Minister, may be different. The Conservatives had no comparable party meeting until 1922; since then its "1922 Committee" (the Conservative and Unionist Members' Committee) has flourished as a sounding board of backbench opinion. When the party is in office it is composed of Commons backbenchers, but ministers may address its weekly meetings. Votes are not usually taken. There is an executive committee of eighteen.

Now that voting in the divisions of the House of Commons has become almost a formality, the party meetings have increased in importance since it is here that MPs can express privately views which might weaken the standing of the party if presented in open debate. Many of those who lament the decline of the Commons condemn private party meetings for being undemocratic. An interesting feature of both main parties is the existence of about 20 party committees in each to study a wide range of subjects from agriculture to aviation. In a sense, these party committees compensate for the absence of specialist committees in Parliament itself. But here again, critics allege that important debates are being conducted in private.

The parliamentary parties have a third role in addition to being disciplined organizations and ideological groupings: they select a Leader who may be the next Prime Minister. The Labour party's Leader is elected by House of Commons members of the parliamentary Labour party and is re-elected annually unless he is Prime Minister of the party in power. There is a maximum of two ballots, so that in the 1963 three-cornered contest of Wilson (115 votes), Brown (88), and Callaghan (41), there was a run-off between Wilson and Brown which Wilson won by 144 to 103. (Later in 1964 when Mr. Wilson became Prime Minister he established the new Department of Economic Affairs for Mr. Brown and made Mr. Callaghan Chancellor of the Exchequer.)

A new procedure for the selection of the Conservative party's Leader was announced in February 1965 partly as a consequence of the furore surrounding the "emergence" of Sir Alec Douglas-Home as Mr. Macmillan's successor when the latter resigned at the time of the 1963 Party Conference. In July 1965, when the party leadership fell vacant, it was filled at an election by Conservative MPs. (If necessary there could have been up to three ballots, the preferential voting system being used in the third.) The successful candidate, Edward Heath, was presented to a meeting of Conservative members of both houses, prospective candidates, and the Executive Committee of the National Union of Conservative and Unionist Associations.

This suggests that the traditional concept of the Conservative party as an organism from which a new head mysteriously emerges is being replaced by that of a machine publicly conducting elections after the manner of the Labour party. Until very recently the Conservative party, which has existed in one form or another since the seventeenth century, seemed to share some of the characteristics of an interest of the realm. The Labour party, a modern institution formed originally outside Parliament, had always shared certain attributes of pressure groups. Foreign observers often failed to notice this qualitative difference, which helps to explain why the Conservatives have regarded themselves as the governing party and why the Labour party has sometimes found the responsibilities of government difficult to maintain. With Mr. Heath's election as Conservative Leader to oppose Mr. Wilson both parties had replaced private-school men of the upper or upper-middle classes by products of local high schools who had won scholarships to Oxford and whose careers depended on ability rather than connections.

In all three parties it is the parliamentary party which not only selects the Leader who becomes Prime Minister but which produces out of its ranks the other executive officers whom the Prime Minister appoints to his Cabinet. The Prime Minister may try to have a free hand, but he is limited in his choice because of his dependence on his followers and because of the facts of political life; certain senior MPs simply must be included in the Cabinet, e.g., Mr. R. A. Butler, who served under Chamberlain, Churchill, Eden, Macmillan, and Douglas-Home. And a defeated Prime Minister does not disappear into private life. He becomes Leader of Her Majesty's Opposition and receives a salary of $3500 in addition to his salary as an MP.

The invention of Her Majesty's Opposition whereby a man is paid a large salary to attack on all possible occasions the actions of another man (the Prime Minister, who is paid an even larger salary) is a unique British contribution to modern political democracy. At the same time the Leader of the Opposition, together with another paid member of the Opposition (his Chief Whip), to say nothng of their counterparts in the Lords, is also paid for welding such opposition into an effective body for the sole purpose of overthrowing the Government. Furthermore, while the Prime Minister and his ministers are liable to have their salaries subjected to discussion and vote in the House, no such course of action is open for the Leader of the Opposition, his salary being borne on the Consolidated Fund, i.e., not subject to annual review.

The voters play a limited role in selecting party leaders. Few know the merits of politicians; their qualities emerge in Parliament and their ministerial future lies in their capacity to convince their parliamentary colleagues (not the voters) of their ability. Very rarely does an MP go to his constituents for support; either his parliamentary party, particularly its leadership, approves of him or it does not. Both the presidential and parliamentary systems subject potential leaders to severe preliminary tests. Neither is in principle superior to the other, but executive power in Britain is secured by climbing the legislative ladder.

This makes many of the peculiarities of British parliamentary life—particularly the relative impotence of parliamentary com-

mittees—more comprehensible. Rather than looking to a committee chairmanship as the prize, an MP looks to a post in the
Government. Therefore few able MPs devote their energies to
improving the committee system. This does not mean that MPs
are tempted to be yes-men. The road to the top involves a willingness to be different, to speak one's mind and to defy the leadership. But the most successful politicians (and often the most
responsible) are those who can calculate nicely when it is advis-
able to be different, when it is worth while to speak one's mind
and when it is essential to defy the leaders. Those who miscalcu-
late may remain perpetual rebels or gadflies. Those who prefer
committee work to the limelight of the chamber may have private
influence, but they exercise little public power.

NATIONAL PARTIES

Each political party has a national organization as well as a
parliamentary party, the headquarters of each party being in
London. Of primary importance for all parties is the control of
the national organization, whether of the central office, the area
federations, or the local constituency arrangements. (The national
party leader is of course elected by the parliamentary party.)
Now that MPs no longer pay their own election expenses, the
raising of money is an important responsibility of the national
organization. Selection of candidates for Parliament and the can-
vassing of electors remains the responsibility primarily of constituency associations.

The Conservative party Leader has more personal authority
than his Labour rival. He has final responsibility for party policy;
he does not attend the Party Conference (though he addresses
it after its formal adjournment); he is not subject to periodic
re-election; he chooses his own shadow cabinet; and he is in
complete charge of party headquarters. However, these formidable powers are exercised only with the consent of the party, as
several leaders have discovered.

The Labour Leader implements, as far as possible, the programme determined jointly by the parliamentary Labour party
and the mass party organization; he reports to the annual party

conference on the work done in Parliament; he is re-elected annually except when Prime Minister; his shadow cabinet is chosen by the parliamentary Labour party; and the party's National Executive Committee directs the party's headquarters.

Thus whereas the Conservative Central Office under its Chairman and General Director is entirely the creature of the Leader, the Labour party's central office, called Transport House, is under a general secretary responsible not to the Leader but to the National Executive Committee. The composition of this body reflects the composition of the party with its affiliated organizations having more power than individual members or even the constituency organizations.

Table 9.1. The National Executive Committee of the
Labour Party

Leader and Deputy Leader (ex officio)
26 members elected at the party conference:

> Treasurer by the conference
> 12 trade union delegates
> 7 constituency party and federation delegates
> 1 delegate of socialist, cooperative and
> professional organizations
> 5 women members elected by the conference

The annual Labour Party Conference, which is generally thought to be more influential than its Conservative counterpart, is less democratic than it looks. By means of the "block vote" representatives of the larger trade unions are able to outvote the constituency representatives, who have often tended to be more radical in their views.

The main difference between the national organizations of the Conservative and Liberal parties on the one hand and that of the Labour party on the other is that the former depend mainly on individual members at constituency and area federation level as well as at the annual conference, while the latter has representatives of affiliated organizations at all levels. The national structure of the Labour party may be described as indirect rather than direct. It is through the affiliation system that the Labour party raises most of its money, and many of its MPs are sponsored by such an organization. Not all affiliated organizations are trade unions. Intellectual groups (like the Fabian Society) and the Co-operative Movement play an important part in the party.

Money is raised locally by all parties for constituency expenses and the local election campaign. The costs of the national campaign are borne by the central offices, which raise large sums from trade unions (the Labour party) and businessmen (the Conservative party). In May, 1964 the Labour party's election fund stood at £755,000, of which £740,000 had been raised by the trade unions.

Although local constituencies do not expect to raise a great deal of money from their individual members, they rely on voluntary helpers to canvass the electors on polling day and during the short campaign which precedes it. The other main task of the local constituencies is the nomination of parliamentary candidates. Complaints are often made that both parties nominate "carpetbaggers" from the Standing Advisory Committee on Candidates (the Conservatives) or from an affiliated organization (the Labour party—never called Laborites in England), but there are numerous examples of constituencies which select their own candidate. In the Labour party, individuals may not submit their own names and the selected candidate requires the endorsement of the National Executive Committee.

The Main Differences Between the Parties

All the political parties have various common elements. In particular there is both a national party which fights elections and a parliamentary party which after an election carries the responsibility of party leadership. The national party has a central office which gives it some power between elections when otherwise the parliamentary party would have complete control of affairs. On the other hand, the parliamentary party has a leader who may also be in charge of the national organization and is certainly the accepted link between the two. A successful party must have mutual confidence between parliamentary party, national party, and the party head office and leader. And all four must be in touch with public opinion. The visitor to London who is interested in politics may visit the Conservative Central Office in Smith Square or the Labour party's headquarters at Transport House knowing that here is the nerve center for the whole party organization.

There are two obvious differences between the Conservative and Labour parties. In social composition the Conservatives tend to represent the upper, middle, and lower middle classes, and in the House of Commons the Conservative members are predominantly middle and upper class. Most speak with cultivated accents. The Labour party, on the other hand, while it draws many of its leaders from traditional "governing classes" (John Strachey's family helped to govern India: Hugh Gaitskell had a brother in the Sudan: Hugh Dalton's father was chaplain to the King) contains a fair number of lower middle class trade union officials and several who proudly insist they are part of the working class. The Liberals are different again in social composition. They have a sprinkling of Etonians but give the impression of depending on the "new" middle class, whatever this may mean—the TV personality rather than the lawyer, the salaried organization man rather than the independent businessman. They are nearer the Conservatives than the Labour party in the nature of their support and in the appearance of their few MPs. In 1965 *The Manchester Guardian Weekly* reported that the Conservative MPs included 83 company directors, 64 barristers, 43 farmers, 31 journalists or publicists, 16 retired regular officers of the armed forces, and 14 "businessmen." The parliamentary Labour party had 46 teachers, 43 trade union officials, 42 journalists and publicists, 32 barristers, 29 businessmen, 24 industrial workers, and 21 coalminers. The newspaper commented that both parties were obviously short of scientists and engineers and that this was a pity.

The second difference is in programme. To say that the Labour party has a socialist ideology and that the Conservatives favor free enterprise, while tempting to many Americans puzzled by the subtleties of European politics, is a gross oversimplification. The Labour party, as the Communists never tire of pointing out, has abandoned much of its socialist doctrine and far from wishing to implement Clause 4 of its Constitution ("the common ownership of the means of production, distribution and exchange") is in fact reduced to vague talk of giving "the community power over the commanding heights of the economy," heights which have been firmly held by every Government since 1940. Eighty percent of British industry remains in private hands and seems likely to remain so, even if the steel industry is nationalized again.

The Conservatives of course claim to be the party of free enterprise, but this is not exactly true either. A section of the party has always been somewhat suspicious of the business community ever since the Tories represented the landed classes in the days when the rising bourgeoisie were Liberals. It has never hesitated to appeal to the workers if the national interest seems to demand it, and it has protected the farmers and favored the aristocracy. The "free enterprise" American business elements have had little counterpart in Britain since the decline of the Liberals, and the Conservatives are as prone to favor government intervention as the Labour party—but on paternalist grounds. The controversy over the introduction of commercial television in the 1950s severely strained the cohesion of the Conservatives, and at least in the short run the free enterprisers won the day—led by John Profumo. But they suffered when he was disgraced in 1963 and Ian Macleod, their leading spokesman, was unsuccessful in furthering the candidature of either Mr. Butler or himself. Sir Alec Douglas-Home typified the more traditional type of Conservative leader, and no one would say he was a businessman or a representative of free enterprise.

Hamstrung by the pragmatic stand of both major parties, the Liberals lie uneasily between, proclaiming the nebulous advantages of "ownership for all," a rallying cry which both of their opponents could easily echo, the Labour party meaning community ownership of the commanding heights and the Conservatives home ownership, profit-sharing and so on.

A less publicized difference until fairly recently, and one which is even more difficult to unravel, is in the organization of the parties. The Conservatives are accused of being oligarchic (if not autocratic) in organization. Indeed the "Conservative party" *is* the Conservative body of MPs, candidates, and peers. The national party is called the National Union of Conservative and Unionist Associations. The "autocracy" is said to be the result of allowing the control of the Central Office to be solely with the Leader. Nothing is thought to demonstrate the *fuhrerprinzip* more than the spectacle of the annual Party Conference. Since only after it is over does the Leader appear before the assembled delegates to survey national policy.

In practice the Conservative party is much more attuned to (and influenced by) public opinion than is generally realized. The peculiar machinations in 1957 and 1963 before a new Leader "emerged" were due not only to the operation of a residual oligarchy but to the determination of the elder statesmen to secure a Leader who could be certain of the widest possible support. As for the awe in which the Leader is supposed to be held, it is worth recalling the swiftness with which Conservatives dispatch those Leaders who are thought unsuitable. Robert McKenzie has drawn attention to the "cannibalism" at the top of the party.

The Labour party is apparently democratic in its mode of operation. Not only is the Leader elected by the party conference, and elected annually, but he is directed and controlled in the activity of the party outside Parliament by the National Executive Committee. Even within the parliamentary Labour party, when it is in opposition, there is the elected "shadow Cabinet." All this is very different from Conservative political behavior. The public quarrels within the Labour party and the balloting for a new Leader have all been indications of a difference in style. If conservative politics (until 1965) suggest the continuation of a medieval and organic tradition in British politics, overlaid with the ruthless capacity to select and dismiss its leaders which any political party must have if it is to survive in the present age, then the Labour party represents Britain's concession to the democratic and pluralist temper of modern times.

But in practice the Labour party is not quite so democratic as it appears. It is true that the Leader is acclaimed annually at the Party Conference but first he is elected by his colleagues in the parliamentary Labour party. Admittedly, in contrast to the Conservatives, the term "Labour party" means the national party, so much so that the term parliamentary Labour party has to be used (one does not speak of the parliamentary Conservative party), but the Conference always accepts the parliamentary group's choice and always re-elects him. It is also true that the National Executive Committee has power over the national party, but the main decisions are taken in Parliament and the national party has not been able to reduce the parliamentary Labour party to the position of being its parliamentary mouthpiece. And within the House of Commons the Leader enjoys great prestige and power. As Premier the Leader alone appoints his own ministers. The party was shocked when Ramsay MacDonald first adopted this traditional practice of British Prime Ministers and in the early 1930s registered its disapproval of his conduct. But in 1945 Mr. Attlee and in 1964 Mr. Wilson behaved in exactly the same way. There is no indication that the parliamentary party will take the step of electing ministers on the Australian model.

Finally, we may recall that the Labour Party Conference and indeed the parliamentary Labour party are not really "democratic" bodies. The conference represents both passive trade unionists and active local party workers. The voting rules enable the leaders of the large unions to use the "block vote" whereby a single delegate can put up his hand and vote on behalf of the million-odd members of the Transport and General Workers' Union of which he is General Secretary, easily outvoting the entire constituency representation. In the House of Commons itself many members owe their election to the nomination of a trade union or cooperative society which pays their election expenses (and often an additional salary as well). Such MPs may not act as responsible individuals in the election of the party Leader.

One fact does stand out in the postwar era. The Labour party has depended very much on the grass-roots morale of the workers and on the confidence of the working men in factory, mine and workshop in men of their own kind who have represented them. Until the 1964 election it paid less attention to advertising, public relations, and TV publicity—the "gimmicks of the bosses" directed at the consumer and the housewife. In an age of advertising, particularly on TV, this has meant giving the Conservatives a great advantage because they have always relied much more on propaganda lavishly financed from the Central Office. And with the decline of grass-roots ardor, of trade unions, Nonconformity and class consciousness, the Labour party in the affluent society has had the worst of both worlds.

We have already seen that the Liberals have drawn support from white-collar individuals who have felt neglected in the political and economic dialogue between management and labor. These individuals are not organized like their opponents, but they have votes, and in 1964 over 3 million people voted Liberal.

How, then, shall we summarize the differences between the parties? The Conservatives may seem to be a semifeudal club and the Labour party to be more a collection of disparate democrats. In practice the Conservatives are anything but reactionary, while the Labour party is a pseudo-democracy. Yet it is the Labour party which has tried to be democratic in political terms; the Conservative party, as befits a party financed by businessmen, has geared its oligarchic organization to the demands of the consumers of its policies. There is something attractive in the Labour party's dogged attempts to live up to its traditional ideals; but the Conservatives, for all their apparent lack of genuine democratic beliefs, seem to have the capacity to adapt themselves to social change. Curiously enough it is the Conservatives who have often appeared to be the progressive party in tune with the times and the Labour party which has seemed reactionary. But to those Socialists who believe that party policies should be based on doctrine this seems less an indictment of the Labour party than of the times in which they are compelled to live.

In concluding this section on parties we draw attention to three other interesting features of British party life. In the first place, British parties are the prime generators of ideas which ultimately are translated into policy. No one can study the Labour party without being interested in the role of the Fabian Society (though it must be noted that the index of Michael Foot's biography of Aneurin Bevan, Vol. I, contains no reference to the Society); and no one can ignore the Bow Group, a pamphlet-producing group of young progressive Conservatives, in trying to understand the policy of recent Conservative governments. Parties regard themselves as responsible for programmes. In the United States the party "platform" plays a different role, comparable to the flaccid communiqué issued after a meeting of world statesmen. Indeed it is arguable that the function performed by the parties in Britain is carried on in the United States by research divisions attached to the departments and agencies of the executive branch. These produce arguments based less on polemics than on statistics and reflect the differences in style between the politics of the two countries—the oratorical Westminster debate as distinct from the more dispassionate committee analysis of the evidence found in Washington.

Secondly, British parties (even the Conservative party) seem in large measure to depend on volunteers who expect little reward. Such worthwhile patronage as is still available tends to be the reward for those at the top of the organization, whose peerage or baronetcy "for political and public services," including fundraising, carries far more prestige (and is hereditary) than the medal given those at the bottom. No jobs in the civil service or nationalized industries are awarded to the party faithful, yet somehow people remain as interested in politics as ever.

Finally, although most people in Britain seem to vote as they themselves wish and not because any church or trade union or business corporation tells them to vote a certain way, government policy is to some extent dependent on the views held by organizations which supply funds and have access to the party headquarters' machinery. It may be no coincidence that the Conservative party, the party said to be supported by the brewers, should have made one of its first acts after re-election in 1951 the transfer of beer parlors in the new towns from state to private ownership. Not long afterwards a pressure group aided by the Conservative Central Office was able to secure the intro-

duction of commercial television. Unfortunately the inside workings of British politics, owing to the secrecy regarding party funds
and the severity of the libel laws, are still much of a mystery and
it is difficult to assess the relative influence of organized groups on
the one hand and the electors on the other. But groups are sufficiently important to merit a section by themselves.

Groups

PRESSURE GROUPS

There are many organized groups in Britain but attention is
directed more to pressure groups since these clearly have a direct
political role. They tend to fall into a number of categories.

First there are the large employers organized in the Confederation of British Industry, established in 1965 by a merger of the
British Employers Confederation, the National Union of Manufacturers and the Federation of British Industries. Merchants belong to the hundred or so Chambers of Commerce, company
directors (in their private capacity) to the Institute of Directors
and farmers to the National Farmers' Union. So valuable is membership in these organizations that very few employers remain
outside one or another of them. Important in a different sense
are the trade unions, which comprise 10 million workers of whom
8 million are affiliated to the Trades Union Congress (TUC).
Employers and trade unionists in Britain have their headquarters
in the capital, and both are well represented by members of
Parliament.

Not only are these two main groups, management and labor,
tightly organized, but a number of other pressure groups wield
influence. The cooperative movement has 12 million members.
Professional people like doctors and teachers, and government employees, are well organized. To some extent the highly developed political organization of Britain is due to the concentration
of all power in London: in part it is the result of the important
role of the government in the economy, insisting on "pay pauses,"
"wage freezes" and arbitration of disputes.

Table 9.2. British Elections Since 1945

Election	MPs [a] (Total)	Cons. MPs	Cons. Votes	Labour MPs	Labour Votes	Liberal MPs	Liberal Votes
1945	640	213	9,988,306	393	11,995,152	12	2,248,226
1950	625	298	12,502,567	315	13,266,592	9	2,621,548
1951	625	321	13,717,538	295	13,948,605	6	730,556
1955	630	344	13,311,936	277	12,404,970	6	722,405
1959	630	365	13,749,830	258	12,215,538	6	1,638,571
1964	630	303	12,001,396	317	12,205,814	9	3,092,878
1966	630	253	11,418,433	363	13,057,941	12	2,327,533

[a] Not all MPs have belonged to the three main parties, but the number of independents and representatives of other parties has dropped from 22 in 1945 to one (the Speaker) in 1964 and two in 1966.

Table 9.3.   Examples of British Groups

A. *Pressure Groups*

1. Business and Employers [a]
   Federation of British Industries (1916);
   >8,900 firms and 280 trade associations.
   >Includes National Farmers' Union (1908)
   >of 200,000 members.
   British Employers' Confederation (1919);
   >54 employers' organizations.
   National Association of British Manufacturers (1915);
   >5,000 firms and 60 trade associations.
   Association of British Chambers of Commerce (1860);
   >60,000 members, half being manufacturers.
   Institute of Directors (1903);
   >Over 20,000 members.

2. Trade Unions
   596 unions of which 350 are affiliated to
   the Trades Union Congress (1868), membership about
   8,500,000 (1963).

   The biggest are
   Transport and General Workers' Union
   Amalgamated Engineering Union
   National Union of General and Municipal
   Workers
   Union of Shop, Distributive and Allied
   Workers
   National Union of Railwaymen
   National Union of Mineworkers

   Electrical Trades Union

3. Professional Organizations
   British Medical Association
   National Union of Teachers
   National and Local Government
   Officers Association

4. Promotional Groups
   Economic League
   Lords' Day Observance Society
   League against Cruel Sports

Table 9.3.   (*Continued*)

Howard League for Penal Reform
Royal Society for the Prevention
   of Cruelty to Animals
Council for the Preservation of
   Rural England
National Council of Social Service

B. *Interests of the Realm*
  1. Traditional
     City of London
     Oxford and Cambridge Universities
     Church of England
     Royal Society
     The Times
     Inns of Court
     Conservative Party
  2. Modern
     BBC
     Regional Hospital Boards
     National Coal Board
     Port of London Authority
     British Railways
     BOAC

---

[a] Consolidated into the Confederation of British Industry in 1965.

In addition to groups defending special interests there are organizations which come into being to promote special campaigns—against nuclear arms, capital punishment, vivisection, and so on. But these promotional groups are not always active and may die once their cause is won. The other groups remain committed to enlarging their share of the nation's wealth indefinitely and as the Government extends its power (e.g., by nationalization) so these groups increase the scope of their activities.

Groups bring pressure to bear wherever they can and concentrate on those areas where best results can be achieved. Promotional (or "cause") groups often have to be content with operating at the grass roots or through sympathetic MPs. Powerful pressure groups tend to send their representatives to the appropriate government department, where in fact the main decisions are usually made. British commentators seem to approve of the pleasant personal relations between the groups' representatives and their civil service opposite numbers. They even seem to assume that the civil servants are able to deal with the groups as gods on Mount Olympus dealing with supplicants. Perhaps by American standards the civil servants are in a more powerful position, because the House of Commons cannot be persuaded by antagonistic groups to cut the budget of a government department. Nevertheless the textbook assumption that all is well in Whitehall, thanks to a civil service composed of well-trained and permanent career men, may be as fanciful a view of the melée of modern administration as many other stereotyped views of the sedateness of British political life have been shown to be.

Some British political philosophers, unimpressed by the research carried out into the nature of the political process in the last few years, have argued that "political science" is impossible because so much of what goes on is known only to the politicians engaged. This view, which as we have seen has tended to retard the academic investigation of certain aspects of British politics, rightly reminds us that it is one thing to believe that there is important evidence available and another to know what that evidence is. On the other hand it is arguable that recent investigations, including those of Americans like H. H. Wilson, Harry Eckstein, and Samuel Beer, have cast at least some illumination on what were very dark places indeed.

Nevertheless students of the political process would do well to ponder the harsh condemnation of this relatively new academic discipline in *The Nature and Limits of Political Science* by a Cambridge scholar, Maurice Cowling.

The more determined the effort to provide an education in contemporary politics by studying works like Mr. Chapman's *The Profession of Government*, the Rector of Exeter's *Government by Committee*, Dr. Robert McKenzie's *British Political Parties*, Mr. Richards' *Honourable Members*, Mr. David Butler's election studies or the body of writing which emerges from the shadows of Professors Robson and Titmuss at the London School of Economics and Professor

W. J. M. Mackenzie at Manchester, the farther away from any understanding of the deviousness of all political activity are writers (and
teachers) likely to be led.[1]

These writers might of course retort that but for their type of
investigations (e.g., comparison between election-time promises
and actual performance) the British people might be even less
aware of "the deviousness of all political activity." Yet insofar
as we are tempted to assume that in the past we saw politics
through a glass darkly but now see it face to face, then it is as
well to be reminded that certain aspects of public policy may
never be made known to the contemporary world. For example,
it is now known that Walter Bagehot in his classic *The English
Constitution* (1867) misunderstood some of the workings of
British politics in his day. But few would query the value of his
attempt to explain them. Critics like Mr. Cowling may in effect
be pleading for a retention of that organic and largely unknown
political system which is being replaced by an American-style
pluralistic society. (His book, despite its broad title, makes no
reference to American writings.)

Governments would like to go about their business untroubled
by a fractious public opinion, but they are unable to do so.
Through a variety of elements in the political process, notably
elections, parties, and groups, the British people are able to bring
influence to bear on both Westminster and Whitehall. And
while we must never forget that Britain is still a constitutional
monarchy it seems reasonable to have applied the American
notion of the sovereign people and to have devoted two chapters
to the link between government and public opinion.

INTERESTS OF THE REALM

"Interests of the realm" is sometimes thought to be the traditional English expression for what are now called pressure
groups. But the term is best used in a more restricted sense: those
elements of the political system which while outside the immediate civil and military jurisdiction of the Crown may neverthe-

[1] Maurice Cowling, *The Nature and Limits of Political Science*, Cambridge University Press, 1963, p. 21.

less reasonably claim to represent, if only in part, the public interest rather than a private interest. As far as traditional interests of the realm are concerned, there is no clear distinction between public and private interest, partly because in the past society was not then so divided. Of the seven examples listed in Table 9.3, The Times could perhaps be said to be the most private and the City of London the most public. The fact that foreigners often consider The Times an organ of government indicates not so much confusion in their minds as an ambiguity in the role of that newspaper.

Fortunately no such ambiguity mars a comprehension of modern interests of the realm. They are set up by royal charter or act of Parliament (as were many traditional interests) and are considered by economists to be part of the public sector of the economy even though their employees are not civil servants. The felicitous phrase coined by The Manchester Guardian for a group of these interests, the nationalized industries, was "autonomous dukedoms." They are autonomous in the sense that they operate outside the area of continuous government control (no questions on their day-to-day operations may be asked in Parliament), but they remain, like dukedoms in the days of the medieval correspondence of rights and duties, responsible public corporations.

Public corporations, like the BBC and Port of London Authority, existed in Britain long before World War II and were the prototype for the postwar Labour Government's nationalized industries and National Health Service. The Labour party thought its innovations captured the best of both worlds—the initiative of the private sector and the responsibility of the public sector. The new organizations were expected to avoid the selfishness of private corporations and the red tape of the civil service. In many ways they succeeded, and some of the criticisms directed at them should more properly be aimed at the nation's broad economic policies.

It was not foreseen at the time that the Government was setting up large-scale monopolies as the Crown had done centuries ago, but in a modern market (and predominantly capitalist) economy. They were not private companies which although responsive to the laws of supply and demand could act as pressure groups from outside the public sector: they were part of it. Nor were they part of the civil service and therefore wholly within the Government's jurisdiction. The Labour Governments of 1945–1951 set up a new business and professional administrative structure: modern interests of the realm employing millions of people and spending billions of dollars annually. They thought they were putting into practice the principles of democratic socialism.

It is easy to overestimate the extent of "socialism" in Britain. In fact only 10 percent of the working population are in nationalized industries and another 10 percent in government employment. The remainder of the population is still in the private sector. But the impact of these great monopolies on the economy has nevertheless been considerable. Their expenditure is state expenditure and their investment budgets are a heavy drain on the Exchequer. Their employees regard themselves as public servants and therefore entitled to at least standard wages and salaries. Yet their policies are not fully controlled by the Government (if this had been intended they would have been made part of the civil service as they are on the Continent) and are not fully controlled by the market (for if they were then they would be in the same position as private corporations). Although the Labour Government hoped they would have "the best of both worlds" the result has been a certain confusion. The National Coal Board, conscious of its dependence on the goodwill of the National Union of Mineworkers, regards itself as having an obligation to sustain the mining community as well as to provide coal for consumers at reasonable prices. In 1964 it insisted that it had annual fixed costs of over £200 million whatever the level of output, and that if it was not able to sell 200 million tons a year there would inevitably be a rise in the price of coal.

Not all nationalized industries have been in economic difficulty, but those which have been faced by a declining market have been placed in a dilemma. Indeed it is arguable that they have the worst of both worlds. If they adhere strictly to business principles they may benefit the taxpayer but they hurt powerful pressure groups—the National Union of Mineworkers or the National Union of Railwaymen. As part of the public service the nationalized industries are not free to act with the ruthlessness of a private business (though there is evidence that even private corporations, notably in the steel and aircraft industries, have been equally guilty of overstaffing). Consequently they have agreed to higher wages even though they were not making enough money to pay them. In a sense, therefore, their employees have acquired the security of civil servants while retaining the right to strike to enforce their claims. In Chapter Four we saw some of the implications of Britain's willingness to satisfy present consumption at the expense of future investment. How far Britain's problems have been aggravated by the existence of a number of institutions which by virtue of their status as interests of the realm are not governed by the market it is difficult to say, but they have probably contributed to a new way of life which lays less emphasis on profit-making—if only because nationalized industries have been statutorily required only to break even, taking one year with another. Hence, the term "neo-feudalism" has been coined to describe these powerful domestic interests of the realm which have modified Britain's market economy. However, the British economy is so dependent on international trade that it is doubtful whether the country as a whole can insulate itself from the pressures of the international market economy.

Since 1948 the National Health Service has covered doctors, dentists, ophthalmologists, hospitals and local authority services such as ambulances, and home nursing. Unlike the nationalized industries, the Health Service was never intended to depend on payment for services rendered. It was, and is, financed in part by compulsory flat rate contributions by all citizens, but mostly out of taxation in the same way as education. (Until the threat of strike action in 1965 the doctors were a less powerful pressure group than the railwaymen or miners.)

The element in the rather amorphous National Health Service which corresponds most to an interest of the realm is the Regional Hospital Board. The 15 Boards are responsible for 369 Hospital Management Committees which in turn manage nearly 3000 hospitals. Their officers are appointed by the Minister of Health who also provides their funds. The great teaching hospitals, 36 in all, enjoy a separate status under their own Boards of Governors: these ancient institutions, like the City of London, have managed to retain their own identity.

Before 1948 hospitals were either voluntary (i.e., private) or municipal. The NHS Act vested ownership of most of them in the Minister of Health. Yet they are not part of the civil service and though financed from the Exchequer they remained so autonomous that a royal commission had to be set up to inquire into the cost of the National Health Service, including the hospitals. The status of the NHS in general, and the hospitals in particular, is somewhat unclear.

These new interests of the realm, such as hospital boards and nationalized industries which are outside the civil service, have been called "partly independent agencies." [2] Their creation as institutions distinct from the traditional civil service form of organization may seem to demonstrate the impact of the new pluralism on official policy. But the status of these interests as *public* bodies suggests that the organic tradition is still being preserved.

[2] Norman Wilson, *The British System of Government*, Oxford: Basil Blackwell, 1963, Chapter Five.

Conclusion to Part III

In Part III we have analyzed the changing British political system and the shift of power from monarch, Lords, and even Commons to the Cabinet on the one hand and the public on the other. In the sixteenth and seventeenth centuries—and even up to the American Revolutionary War—the British monarch had the power to determine whether or not the country would go to war, the most formidable of powers. The King was head of the body politic. In the eighteenth century the milords of England and their retinues were conspicuous throughout Europe and the House of Lords symbolized their power and prestige. By means of bribery and corruption the Lords controlled a large part of the House of Commons. The British aristocracy formed a powerful oligarchy which provided the sinews of the body politic. Today both parts of the body politic, the monarchy and the House of Lords, are in decay.

By the nineteenth century, despite the strenuous efforts of Queen Victoria, the House of Commons seemed to be supreme and the debates between Gladstone and Disraeli were followed with interest throughout the country. Gladstone's dream of ending or mending the remaining enemy of the Commons, the House of Lords, was fulfilled in 1911 when the Parliament Act statutorily limited its powers. But already the House of Commons was beginning to decline as necessary reforms, resulting in part from the influence of first the Irish members and then the Labour party, transferred power from the House to the Government. By 1937 Ivor Jennings was able to publish his definitive book significantly entitled Cabinet Government and the following year Harold Laski (prematurely) pronounced the obsequies of parliamentary government in England with a book of that title. But though the old organic structure of British politics and society had by no means disappeared it was no longer in full vigor.

Today interest in British politics tends to center on the Government and on parties and groups. People are keenly concerned about the political life of the country outside the House of Commons. There is some uneasiness that the parliamentary tradition is in some ways elitist if not oligarchic and opposed to the new pluralistic political style with its emphasis on extra-parliamentary activity. (It is difficult to imagine a Victorian Premier "going to the country" after examining the latest Gallup poll estimate of his popularity.)

The "new pluralism" tends to be not only American in conception but to owe a great deal to American experience. Until very recently it was widely assumed outside the United States that Old World political behavior was the model and that North American politics were a deviation, possibly temporary, from the norm. Many British and European observers thought that America's belated urbanization would lead to a more organized working class and the development of left-wing political parties. Today it is the experience of the United States and Canada which is often the model for the new affluent middle-class society of modern Europe, an experience which may become even more relevant if the European countries draw together in some supranational organization in any way comparable to the American Union or the Dominion of Canada. (Even the United Nations has been more American than European in its mode of operation.) Europeans have come to recognize with surprise that, far from being backward, Americans have been in the forefront in the extension of the franchise, the growth of national parties, the emergence of pressure groups, and the development of a society dominated by the urban middle class. And so North American writers on British parties and groups are at last finding their conceptual framework taken seriously: American-style pluralism is the most pervasive fact of political life in the Western world today. (Whether it will be equally influential in the non-Western world remains to be seen.)

The British Parliament is caught between an increasingly powerful Government and an increasingly influential public opinion via polls, pressure groups and national party organizations, and is itself in danger of losing its influence, an influence which has on the whole been to the good. For Britain's main contribution to the political experience of the world may well prove to have been the evolution of parliamentary government from the sixteenth to the twentieth century—a contribution which may one day rival that of ancient Athens. Its political style is very different from the American or Continental and may well be unique. As a blend of the old and the new, contemporary British parliamentary government is organic in form and pluralist in content.

PART IV

*Britain in the
Contemporary World*

CHAPTER TEN

Imperial and Foreign Affairs

> *Let us therefore brace ourselves to our*
> *duties, and so bear ourselves that, if*
> *the British Empire and its Common-*
> *wealth last for a thousand years, men*
> *will say: "This was their finest Hour."*
> Winston Churchill
> June 1940

HISTORY may be about to repeat itself. Instead of being the hub
of a great empire Britain may be returning to the role she played
for nearly a thousand years after her history was first recorded by
the Roman writer Tacitus: that of an offshore island 20 miles from
the Eurasian landmass. Successive occupations added to the in-
digenous Celtic and Early British strains those of the Romans,
Angles, Saxons, Jutes, and finally Normans, whose invasion (which
proved to be the last) occurred in 1066. Traces of the Conquest
remain today: the upper classes are proud of their Norman an-
cestry, though less obviously so than before the industrial revolution.[1]

After the thousand years of invasions there was a period of five
hundred years of some intimacy with Europe. The Norman kings
did not abandon their Duchy of Normandy, and England fought
the Hundred Years' War (1337–1453) to retain her possessions
in France. Calais, her last toehold on the Continent, was not
abandoned until 1558, the year of Elizabeth I's accession to the
throne. From then on Britain's eyes were turned from Europe to
the Atlantic and beyond.

[1] Disraeli's novel *Sybil* (1845) assumed a continuing class and ethnic tension between Norman and Saxon.

For the next four hundred years, roughly 1558 to 1940, England was a great sea power colonizing the empty spaces of the world. She defeated the Spanish Armada in 1588, exhausted the Dutch navy in the late seventeenth century, trounced the French at Trafalgar in 1805, and battered the Germans at Jutland in 1916. Unable to dominate Europe, she was pleased to see it divided. She did not participate in the Thirty Years' War (1618–1648) but played an effective part in the War of the Spanish Succession (1701–1714) and the Napoleonic Wars (1803–1815). Her main setback was the revolution in the American colonies which put an end to the First Empire, but even then she was laying the foundations of her Second Empire in Canada and India. In the nineteenth century her people were settling not only in North America but in South Africa, Australia and New Zealand. Her armies and merchants occupied much of Africa, the Middle East and the Far East and her naval bases spanned the globe from Portsmouth to Gibraltar, Halifax, and Singapore. By 1900 Cecil Rhodes could dream of a Cape to Cairo railroad entirely through territory marked red on the map; and at her Diamond Jubilee in 1897 Queen Victoria, Empress of India, surveyed an empire on which the sun never set. Conservative party conferences sang

> Land of Hope and Glory, Mother of the free
> How shall we extol thee, who are born of thee?
> Wider still and wider shall thy bounds be set,
> God who made thee mighty, make thee mightier yet!

And though in 1918 it was unthinkable that Britain should acquire yet more colonies, she nevertheless obtained a number of former German territories which she administered as League of Nations "Mandates." The British Empire had reached its fullest extent. From her Falkland Islands base in the South Atlantic Britain disputed control of Antarctica with Argentina and Chile; in the Far East her gunboats patrolled the Yangtse River in China. (Indeed in 1965 she was still disputing the claim of China and Indonesia to control Malaysia and the eastern seas, concentrating much of what remained of the Royal Navy in the crucial Straits of Malacca.)

Until very recently, Britain's record was one of which the average Englishman was immensely proud. She had kept in being for centuries the largest and most powerful navy in the world; she had developed the largest empire the world had ever seen, and had administered it efficiently and magnanimously before helping to transform it into a self-governing Commonwealth; and for over 700 years she had been perfecting parliamentary institutions which were a political model for the rest of the world. Alone of the Great Powers she had withstood invasion for a thousand years, resisting even Napoleon and Hitler. To many besides Churchill, 1940 was—with the enemy once again held at bay— "Britain's finest hour."

Yet in fact it was the end of an era which had begun in 1558 —or possibly 1066. Having turned outwards from Europe to conquer an empire—taking Quebec and India from the French, New York and South Africa from the Dutch, Caribbean islands and Gibraltar from the Spanish, Egypt and Iraq from the Turks, Tanganyika and South West Africa from the Germans—the British were soon to begin a rapid withdrawal. The transformation of the Empire into a Commonwealth disguised from them the fact that their power was rapidly declining. In 1940 Britain could stand alone against a German-controlled Europe. By 1956 she could not assert herself against the ill-armed Egyptians: the Pax Britannica had given way to the Pax Americana. By 1964 Britain was financially the chronically sick man of Europe. The withdrawal had begun in Asia when the Indian subcontinent achieved independence in 1947. China expelled the British in 1949, and in 1951 the Australian and New Zealanders formed a defensive alliance with the United States. Britain was not a member of the Anzus pact.

In the 1950s the scene shifted to Africa and the Middle East. Britain's control of Middle East oil, for which campaigns had been waged in two world wars, was whittled away following the confrontation with Iran over the Abadan refinery in 1951. With the emancipation of the countries of Africa and the Near East she abandoned her bases first in Suez, then in Kenya and Cyprus one after the other.

Only the "old Dominions" remained untouched. But the emergence of a colored majority among the nations of the Commonwealth led to strained relations, and the notion of a Commonwealth which crossed racial boundaries became a chimera. At an historic meeting of Commonwealth Prime Ministers in 1960 the South Africans were forced to withdraw from the Commonwealth because of *apartheid*. Yet her principal critic, Canada, like Australia and New Zealand, had never permitted free immigration from the colored Commonwealth countries. Only two years later, Britain herself felt constrained to abandon her position as Mother Country, at least as far as colored immigrants were concerned, though not before a million of these had entered. By 1965 the Rhodesian crisis imposed a severe strain on Commonwealth unity.

The countries of the "white Commonwealth" (and particularly their people of British descent) are placed in a dilemma. The English South Africans have had to acquiesce in the setting up of a republic and separation from the Commonwealth as well as *apartheid*. The English Canadians have found themselves caught between a restless French-Canadian minority unwilling to pay homage to the Queen and a powerful neighbor across the border. Increasingly Canada has been reconciling herself to being part of the North American continent rather than being the apex of a North Atlantic triangle. Australia and New Zealand, which provide tempting morsels to the billions of underfed Asians, hope that American power will protect them. Well might some American political scientists refer to British colonists as "the fragment." For even the white Commonwealth, of which the English-Speaking Union was so proud such a short while ago, faces the prospect of ultimate dissolution.

One of the things which holds the Commonwealth, excluding Canada, together is an economic interdependence symbolized by the sterling area. Capital has been raised in London to finance projects throughout the Commonwealth. But as the pound sterling has been weakened the advantages of the sterling area have dwindled and any further devaluation following on the devaluations of 1931 and 1949 could break one of the last tenuous links binding the Commonwealth together.

The once powerful Royal Navy is now small in comparison with the United States Navy. For the United States has taken over Britain's role. The Sixth Fleet has replaced the British Mediterranean Fleet based on Malta; the Seventh Fleet holds the China Station once occupied by the Far East Fleet based on Singapore. The Americans predominate in Middle East oil, in Western defense from the Caribbean to Viet Nam and even in economic aid to many of the developing countries which are part of the Commonwealth. Indeed it is upon American missiles, aircraft, and Polaris submarines that the defense of Britain itself largely rests.

It has been hard for the British to recognize that the developments of the postwar era are viewed abroad as a tragedy for Britain rather than a triumph.[2] Intellectuals in the Labour party have found an outlet for their idealism (and possibly their subconscious paternalism) in concern for the new Commonwealth. African problems in particular have exercised a peculiar fascination over the British mind. (Both parties have been somewhat indifferent to the white dominions.) The Labour party until 1964 fought against restrictions on Commonwealth immigration, whether colored or white. Admittedly many leading Conservatives decided in the late 1950s that Britain's future lay with Europe; but the Labour party fought and won the 1964 election in favor of the Commonwealth instead. This apparent reversal of roles was due in large measure to the emergence of an independent colored Commonwealth in which Conservatives had little interest.

Whether Britain will finally abandon her "responsibilities to the Commonwealth and Empire" remains to be seen. Had she chosen she could have provided leadership for Western European integration after 1945, dominating France as she had tried to do six hundred years earlier. In the 1950s she could have participated in Europe on equal terms with Germany and France. But since DeGaulle's rejection of her application (unless she abandoned Commonwealth preferences) the relations of Britain and

[2] ". . . the history of the past fifteen years has been a prodigious and unparalleled record of decolonization, a record, I'm afraid, which has not always received the acclaim it deserves in the world." Speech by Harold Wilson, 16 November, 1964.

Europe have been uneasy. Financial weakness has transformed Britain into a supplicant, dependent on France and Germany for loans to bolster the pound. What would happen if Britain did join the European Economic Community? Would she take a new lease on life—or would she find that the competition weakened her still further? If she did not join EEC, would she revert to being an offshore island as she was before 1066—though without the stimulus of waves of immigration?

Admiral Mahan, less than 80 years ago, in *The Influence of Seapower on History*, showed how important control of the seas was for any country wishing to be a world power in the seventeenth and eighteenth centuries. But more important today is the size of the industrial population, the extent of domestic natural resources such as gas, oil, lumber (and even water and gold) and the dynamism of a country's science and technology. The USA, USSR, and potentially both continental Europe and ultimately China have these necessary qualities for world influence. Britain alone has not, and her dispersed Commonwealth may not be able to withstand the pressures which the great continental powers are beginning to exercise, whether on the Tibetan border, at Niagara Falls—or even across the Straits of Dover.

Indeed *England's* predominant position in the British Isles could weaken if Scotland and Wales continued to develop their sense of national identity and if Northern Ireland patched up its quarrel with the Irish Republic. Future historians may conclude that English history from the Norman Conquest in 1066 to the Age of Churchill forms a single period, an era when England was independent of the Continent of Europe barely 20 miles away. Within this 900-year span they may trace a smaller epoch: the Age of Empire from Elizabeth I and the victory over the Armada to Elizabeth II and the conquest of Everest, four centuries during which England was able to dominate much of the world through her sea power.

In this book we have been much more concerned with Britain as a parliamentary democracy, proud of a political system which has been for 700 years in a process of evolution, than with Britain in the world. It is an old country and one which has known much adversity and isolation as well as periods of imperial grandeur. It will last for many more centuries to come. The end of empire and the growing dependence of Britain on Europe does not mean the end of Britain as an important influence in the world. This would be to read too much into the recent lessons of history. But there is every indication that her influence will be vastly different from that of the past few centuries.

SELECTED READINGS

Society

Of the many critiques of British society published in the last few years the most comprehensive and illuminating is

SAMPSON, A., *Anatomy of Britain Today*, London: Hodder and Stoughton, 1965.

Constitution

Two standard works are

WADE, E. C. S., and PHILLIPS, G. G., *Constitutional Law*, 7th ed., London: Longmans, 1965.

KEIR, SIR DAVID L., *Constitutional History of Modern Britain Since 1485*, 7th ed., London: A. & C. Black, 1964.

Government

For a standard work

JENNINGS, SIR IVOR, *Cabinet Government*, 3rd ed., Cambridge: University Press, 1959.

A recent study of the development of the Cabinet is

MACKINTOSH, J. P., *The British Cabinet*, London: Stevens, 1962.

For a readable book by a former Cabinet Minister

MORRISON, H., *Government and Parliament*, 3rd ed., London: Oxford University Press, 1964.

Economy

A recent scholarly study is

DOW, J. C. R., *The Management of the British Economy 1945–60*, Cambridge: University Press, 1964.

A more popular book is

SHONFIELD, A., *British Economic Policy*, Harmondsworth: Penguin Books, 1958.

For reference purposes there are

Britain: An Official Handbook, London: Central Office of Information, annually.

Annual Abstract (and *Monthly Digest*) *of Statistics of the United Kingdom*.

Administration

MACKENZIE, W. J. M., and GROVE, J. W., *Central Administration in Great Britain*, London: Longmans, 1957.

JACKSON, R. M., *The Machinery of Local Government*, London: Macmillan, 1958.

JACKSON, R. M., *The Machinery of Justice in England*, 4th ed., Cambridge: University Press, 1964.

The Crown and the House of Lords

NICOLSON, SIR HAROLD, *King George V: His Life and Reign*, London: Constable, 1953.

BROMHEAD, P. A., *The House of Lords and Contemporary Politics 1911–1957*, London: Routledge and Kegan Paul, 1958.

House of Commons

A standard work is

JENNINGS, SIR IVOR, *Parliament*, 2nd ed., Cambridge: University Press, 1957.

A shorter account is found in

TAYLOR, ERIC, *The House of Commons at Work*, rev. ed., Harmondsworth: Penguin Books, 1963.

Elections and the Electorate

There are studies of every general election since 1945, the most recent being

BUTLER, D. E., and ROSE, R., *The British General Election of 1959*, London: Macmillan, 1960.

BUTLER, D. E., and KING, A., *The British General Election of 1964*, London: Macmillan, 1965.

For the electoral system see

BUTLER, D. E., *The Electoral System in Britain since 1918*, 2nd ed., Oxford: Clarendon Press, 1963.

BLONDEL, J., *Voters, Parties and Leaders*, Harmondsworth: Penguin Books, 1963.

Parties, Pressure Groups and Interests of the Realm

The standard work on parties is

MCKENZIE, R. T., *British Political Parties*, 2nd rev. ed., London: Mercury Books, 1964.

A recent American sociological analysis is

ROSE, R., *Politics in England*, Boston: Little, Brown, 1964.

For a specific pressure group see

WILSON, H. H., *Pressure Group: the campaign for commercial television in England*, New Brunswick, N.J.: Rutgers University Press, 1961.
On interests of the realm see SAMPSON, A., noted under Society.

Britain in the Contemporary World

STRACHEY, JOHN, *The End of Empire*, London: Gollancz, 1959.
Keesing's Contemporary Archives (continuous).

Reference

BAGEHOT, W., *The English Constitution* (1867), new edition, London: Watts, 1964. Besides having a useful introduction by R. H. S. Crossman, it contains a comprehensive bibliography on British Central Government and Politics by Colin Seymour-Ure.

BUTLER, D. E., and FREEMAN, JENNIE, *British Political Facts 1900–1960*, London: Macmillan, 1963.

Whitaker's Almanack (annual)

WILDING, N., and LAUNDY, P., *An Encyclopaedia of Parliament*, 2nd rev. ed., London: Cassell, 1961.

INDEX